No Ordinary R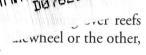

"We were six days going from St.
boat might almost as well have gor.
was walking most of the time, an)   ...er reefs
and clambering over snags, with one   ...wheel or the other,
patiently and laboriously all day long."

—MARK TWAIN, *ROUGHING IT*

"July 26 [1867]—Started at 3 A.M., and after running about
40 miles stopped to wood on right bank; on starting out again
encountered a sudden and very severe storm and blow, which
forced us to the bank for an hour, during which time a cottonwood tree of one foot diameter was blown across the boat in
rear of the cabin, breaking our larboard hog-chains and crushing through a portion of the boiler deck. The storm ceased as
suddenly as it began, and after clearing away the fallen tree we
ran a few hundred yards up the river and tied up alongside a
cut bank to repair.

When we lay up, the bank was cutting slowly, but soon
began to fall in so fast as to make our position dangerous: tons
of earth and willows falling frequently on the lower deck and
threatening to sink the boat. We lay at this place for half an
hour when the small cottonwood to which we had tied 100
feet from the bank was washed in, and we were obliged to
move to a better anchorage, which we found three miles above,
where we lay for the night.

July 27—Although our repairs were not completed this morning, we were obliged to run higher for wood. We lay by all day
wooding and repairing the damage of yesterday. In the afternoon a hurricane came up from the north-northwest and continued until late at night, with occasional lulls and heavy
storms. The air was filled with clouds of sand, and the water
was full of grasshoppers blown off shore."

—JOURNAL OF CAPTAIN C.W. HOWELL
U.S. ARMY CORPS OF ENGINEERS

"These facts lead us naturally to the subject of the Missouri's appetite. It is the hungriest river ever created. It is eating all the time—eating yellow clay banks and cornfields, eighty acres at a mouthful; winding up its banquet with a truck garden and picking its teeth with the timbers of a big red barn. Its yearly menu is ten thousand acres of good rich farming land, several miles of railroad, a few hundred houses, a forest or two, and uncounted miles of sandbars. Throw a man into the Missouri and he will not often drown. It is more likely that he will break his leg."
—GEORGE FITCH, *AMERICAN MAGAZINE*, 1907

"To look at it, some people would think it was just a plain river running along in its bed at the same speed; but it ain't. The crookedness you can see ain't half the crookedness there is."
—CHARLES STEWART, *THE CENTURY MAGAZINE*, 1907

"Any man who can run a boat for twenty years in that rainwater creek above Bismarck is surely the king of pilots."
—HORACE BIXBY, MARK TWAIN'S MENTOR

"We used to separate the men from the boys at the mouth of the Missouri. The boys went up the Mississippi and the men up the Big Muddy."
—"STEAMBOAT BILL" HECKMANN

Wild River, Wooden Boats

TRUE STORIES
OF STEAMBOATING
AND THE
MISSOURI RIVER

by

Michael Gillespie

HERITAGE PRESS
Rt. 1, Stoddard, WI 54658
www.greatriver.com

Published by
Heritage Press
Rt. 1, Stoddard, WI 54658
608-457-2734

On the internet, visit **www.greatriver.com**

ISBN 978-0-9620823-7-5

Library of Congress Catalogue Card Number: 00-130051

08   10 9 8 7 6 5

Design by Sue Knopf, Graffolio, La Crosse, Wisconsin

For my children…
Suzanne
Thomas
Stephen
Deborah
Andrew
Patrick
Mary

Contents

Illustrations and Photographs

At each end of the boats there was a
small deck, under these we stowed
our provisions, etc.; next to the decks
were piled the packs of skins,
secured by ropes, and in the middle
a space of about twelve feet long
was left for the oarsmen.

JOHN BRADBURY, 1811

Prologue:
Before Steam

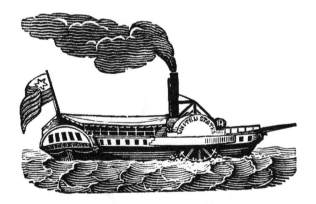

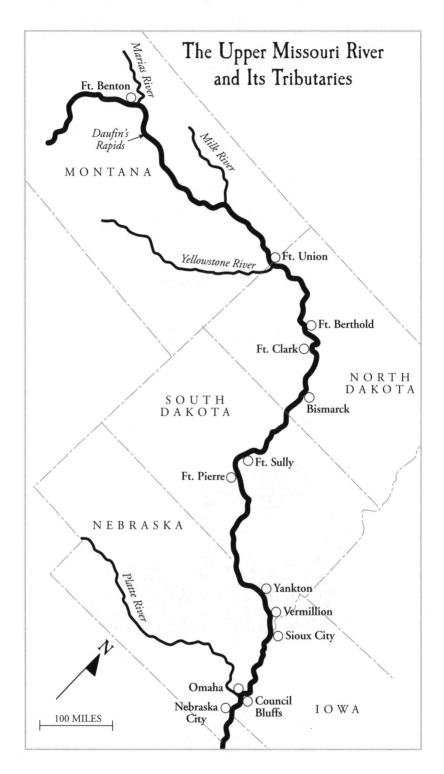

The Upper Missouri River
and Its Tributaries

Marias River

Ft. Benton

Daufin's
Rapids

Milk River

MONTANA

Yellowstone River

Ft. Union

Ft. Berthold

Ft. Clark

NORTH
DAKOTA

SOUTH
DAKOTA

Bismarck

Ft. Sully

Ft. Pierre

NEBRASKA

Platte River

Yankton

Vermillion

Sioux City

N

Omaha

Nebraska
City

Council
Bluffs

IOWA

100 MILES

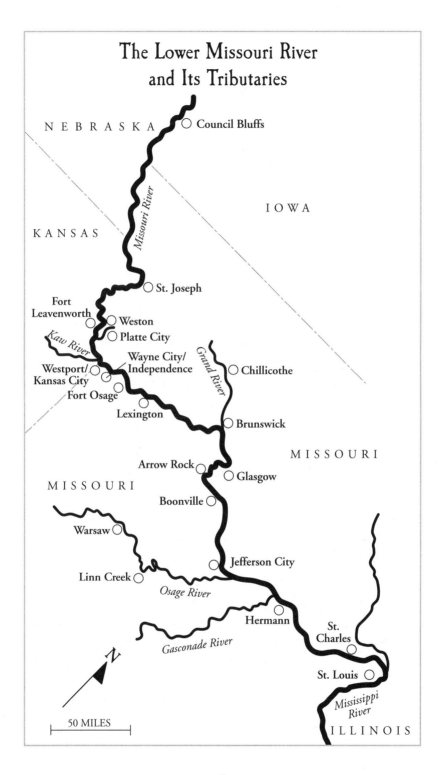

The Lower Missouri River and Its Tributaries

NEBRASKA

O Council Bluffs

IOWA

KANSAS

Missouri River

O St. Joseph

Fort
Leavenworth

Kaw River

O Weston

O Platte City

Wayne City/
Independence

Grand River

O Chillicothe

Westport/
Kansas City

Fort Osage

O Brunswick

Lexington

MISSOURI

Arrow Rock O

O Glasgow

MISSOURI

Boonville O

Warsaw O

Jefferson City O

Linn Creek O

Osage River

Hermann O

St.
Charles

Gasconade River

St. Louis O

Mississippi River

N

ILLINOIS

50 MILES

Discovery

The first European to lay eyes on the Missouri River and leave a record of his journey was the French missionary priest, Jacques Marquette. It caught him unprepared. He and his party had been paddling down the Wisconsin and Upper Mississippi Rivers for weeks and perhaps he was lulled into thinking that the rivers of the Central Basin, though large, were quite benign. The Indians told him to expect a great river coming in from the west—one they called Pekitanoui. They may also have described it as a river with an *attitude,* but if they did the meaning was lost on the good father. So on that June day in 1673 when Marquette finally reached the mouth of the Pekitanoui he was shocked by what he saw. In his journal he wrote:

> As we were gently sailing down the still clear water [of the Mississippi], we heard a noise of a rapid into which we were about to fall. I have seen nothing more frightful, a mass of large trees entire with branches, real floating islands came from Pekitanoui, so impetuous that we could not without great danger expose ourselves to pass across. The agitation was so great that the water was all muddy, and could not get clear.

The Mississippi could not get clear of it, either: from there to the Gulf of Mexico it was a changed river, having picked up all the bad habits of its wild Western cousin. The Missouri River, sired by an ancient glacier and nursed by every raging thunderstorm and howling blizzard that ever crossed the plains at last had been discovered. But discovering the Missouri was somewhat akin to discovering a wildcat in the basement—what does one do with the prize?

The fur trade

From colonial times to the Victorian age, fur trading was a principal commercial enterprise of the frontier. Indians used furs to trade for the white man's manufactured goods. Those furs, especially beaver pelts, were good as gold to the white traders because of a strong demand dictated by fashion trends in Europe. Men grew rich from the fur business, though it was a risky business and many a trapper or trader lost his scalp in the quest.

Fur-bearing animals were found in greatest abundance in those places most distant from the settlements. Whether it was buffalo on the plains or beaver in the mountains, it took hard traveling, skill, and luck to get to them—or to the Indians who hunted them. The Missouri River was the only natural highway to and from the West. In a geographic sense it was ideally situated to handle the fur business.

Ideally situated was one thing, but ideally suited was another. The untamed Missouri was as close to a living thing as a river could get. And it seemed very disinclined to become a highway of commerce. The strength of its current was always an obstacle, but only the most obvious. The Missouri either was too high, too low, too changeable, too menacing, too crooked, too wide, too shallow, or too obstructed to easily serve the purposes of trade and expansion. Yet it was the only way. So red and white men alike slowly adapted their boats to fit the river.

Bullboats, Mackinaws, and keelboats

The Indians developed two craft for use on the Missouri. One was the bullboat, a vessel made of buffalo bull hide stretched across a framework of willow branches. These light craft were easy to propel with a pole, but absorbed water through the skin and had to be drained and dried out every night. Depending on their size, several bullboats could be strung together in a chain and towed by one or two people. Bullboats often were seen on the Platte River, where strong winds blew hard from the southwest and spread out the water to leeward. It was common to tie up on the downwind shore in the evening, only to find the wind had subsided overnight and the shrunken river was half a mile away. The other craft was the dugout canoe—a hollowed out tree trunk with a taper on either end. Dugouts varied in size though generally they could accommodate two oarsmen. Their great advantage was durability—they were just as rugged as the driftwood coming down the river. Both bullboats and dugouts could float in shallow tributary waters and were used extensively in getting bundles of furs down creeks and small rivers to the Missouri itself.

Once on the Missouri the furs could be loaded onto Mackinaw boats. These Mackinaws were flat-bottomed scows with rakish prows and sterns. Measuring perhaps forty feet in length and ten feet in beam, they floated down river with the aid of poles and rudder. They were products of the forests that lined the shores of the middle river and when their downstream trip ended they were taken apart and sold for lumber.

The human-powered boat of preference on the Missouri was the keelboat. Resembling the common depictions of an ark, keelboats featured a rounded bottom built upon a slightly protruded keel, with a pointed bow and stern. They were meant to travel upriver as well as down, and to last for several seasons. On their upstream journey they carried trade goods, on the down trip they freighted furs. They could be quite large—sixty to seventy feet long—and were capable of transporting heavy loads. Most keelboats had an enclosed cabin amidships. Keelboats were rowed, towed, or pushed ahead by poles. Along each side was a platform gangway used for poling. The crew would start at the bow with one end of the poles braced against their shoulders and the other end on the river bottom. On command, the crewmen pushed on the poles and shoved the boat forward while they walked aft on the platform. When the current was too much for poling or rowing, the boat would have to be towed, or cordelled, from shore. Often the shores were so littered with dead trees and driftwood that the towing crew would have to take to the water, and wade forward while pulling the heavy cordelle line.

A MISSOURI RIVER KEELBOAT. Keelboats were expensive to build and meant to last several seasons. Many were given names. This drawing depicts a typical upstream trip with crewmen onshore towing by cordelle while others on board use poles to keep the boat from running too close to the bank.
(COURTESY JEFFERSON NATIONAL EXPANSION MEMORIAL, NATIONAL PARK SERVICE.)

Sometimes nothing worked against the current. British botanist John Bradbury recorded such occasions in his journal of a trip up the Missouri in 1811:

> The navigation had been very difficult for some days, on account of the frequent occurrence of what is termed by the boatmen *embarras*. They are formed by large trees falling into the river, where it has undermined the banks; some of these trees remain still attached by their roots to the firm ground, and the driftwood being collected by the branches, a dam of the length of the tree is formed, round the point of which the water runs with such velocity, that in many instances it is impossible to stem it. On account of these obstacles, we were frequently under the necessity of crossing the river.

Going downstream, keelboats navigated much the same way as Mackinaws. But the larger, heavier keelboats gave their crew more trouble, especially in high water. Bradbury again relates:

> At every sudden turn the momentum of the boats had a continual tendency to throw them ashore on the outer bank, which it required all the skill of the steersman, and strength of the oarsmen, to prevent. In two instances we were very near being carried into the woods, in places where the river overflowed its banks.

Bradbury was more interested in keeping a botanical record of his Missouri River journey than writing a log of a keelboat trip. But he departed from his usual observations to include an account of the more harrowing experiences of keelboating, such as the following adventure that took place a little below White River in present-day South Dakota:

> As the evening approached we noticed a succession of flashes of lightning, just appearing over the bluffs, on the opposite side of the river. This did not for some time excite much attention, as it was by no means an uncommon occurrence; but we soon began to apprehend impending danger, as we perceived that the storm advanced with great rapidity, accompanied with appearances truly terrific. The cloud was of a pitch blackness, and so dense as to resemble a solid body, out of which, at short

intervals, the lightning poured in a stream of one or two seconds in duration. It was too late to cross the river, and unfortunately for us, the side on which we were was entirely bounded by rocks. We looked most anxiously for some little harbour, or jutting point, beyond which we might shelter ourselves; but not one appeared, and darkness came on with a rapidity I never before witnessed. It was not long that any choice was left to us. We plainly heard the storm coming. We stopped and fastened our boats to some shrubs…which grew in abundance out of the clefts of these rocks, and prepared to save ourselves and our little barks if possible. At each end of the boats there was a small deck, under these we stowed our provisions, etc.; next to the decks were piled the packs of skins, secured by ropes, and in the middle a space of about twelve feet long was left for the oarsmen.

Fortunately for us we had some broad boards in each boat, designed as a defense against arrows, had we been attacked by the Sioux. These boards we placed on the gunwale of the boats, and crammed our blankets into such parts as the lightning enabled us at intervals to see did not fit closely. Before we had time to lash our boards the gale commenced, and in a few minutes the swell was tremendous. For nearly an hour it required the utmost exertion of our strength to hold the boards to their places, and before the storm abated we were nearly exhausted, as also were those who were occupied in bailing. As the river is in this place nearly a mile in breadth, and being on the lee shore, the waves were of considerable magnitude, and frequently broke over the boats. Had our fastenings given way, we must inevitably have perished. When the wind abated the rain increased, and continued for the greater part of the night, during which my friend [Henry M.] Brackenridge and myself lay on the deck, rolled up in our wet blankets, congratulating ourselves on our escape.

Travel up and down the Missouri in the days before steam took time. Going up, the pace rarely was faster than a person could walk. Experienced keelboatmen looked for any advantage the begrudging river might give them. Crews sought the backeddies, or sucks—areas below a point where the water formed a long, slow whirlpool. There the inshore current ran upstream and the current would pull the boat up with it. Otherwise the steersman always headed for slack water, provided the depth was adequate. Bullboats, Mackinaws, and keelboats all had masts (if the overhanging trees didn't snap them off) and they carried a sail to rig on the mast. But the course of the Missouri was so crooked that sails normally were of benefit only on a few reaches. The fastest upstream keelboat trip averaged eighteen miles a day. It was an impressive rate, and would compare well with the speed of the earliest steamers, but it was the exception rather than the rule. In the same year that Bradbury recorded his keelboat journey—1811—the first steamboat on the Western Rivers made its inaugural journey down the Ohio and Mississippi Rivers and ushered in the heady days of steamboating.

1

Steamboat Design & Operation

Typical Deck Layout

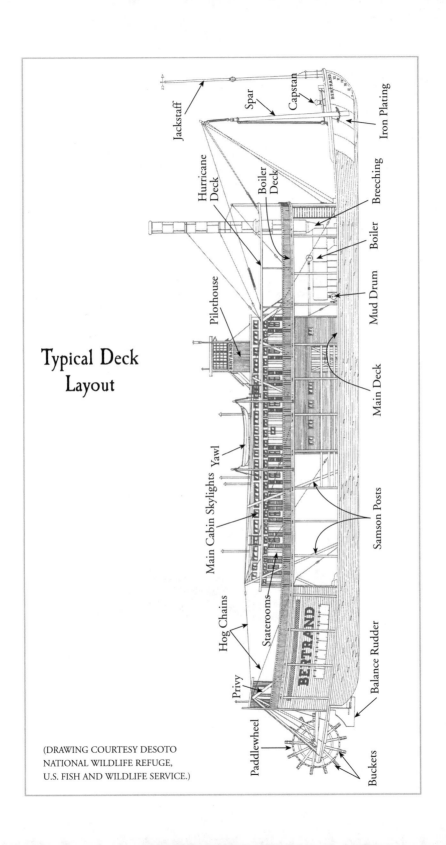

Jackstaff

Spar

Capstan

Iron Plating

Hurricane Deck

Boiler Deck

Breeching

Boiler

Mud Drum

Pilothouse

Main Deck

Main Cabin Skylights

Yawl

Samson Posts

Hog Chains

Staterooms

Privy

Balance Rudder

Paddlewheel

Buckets

(DRAWING COURTESY DESOTO
NATIONAL WILDLIFE REFUGE,
U.S. FISH AND WILDLIFE SERVICE.)

The voyage of the New Orleans

The first steamboat on the Western Rivers—the rivers that comprised the Central Basin of the United States—was designed and built at Pittsburgh in 1810. By most descriptions the boat was 148 feet long by thirty-two feet wide. She was schooner-rigged with two masts and a bowsprit. Apparently her designer, Robert Fulton, thought it prudent to include sails in case the steam apparatus failed. A helmsman steered the vessel by means of a tiller located at the stern; the pilot positioned himself at the bow and directed the helmsman with hand signals.

The engine, mounted vertically in the hold, utilized low-pressure steam and an exhaust-cooling condenser. Some thirty pounds of steam pressure on one side of the piston stroke, enhanced by a partial vacuum on the other, provided power for perhaps twenty revolutions per minute. The piston rod extended upwards, straight through the main deck, where it connected to a fulcrum, known as a walking beam. Another rod, on the opposite end of the beam, reached down to a horizontal crankshaft and converted the up-and-down movements of the walking beam to the circular motions of the shaft. Both ends of the crankshaft extended outboard of the hull, where the arms of the paddlewheels radiated outward. The paddles, or buckets, dug into and out of the water thus propelling the craft. The boiler provided the steam, or "elastic vapor." It was nothing more than an iron cylinder with a firebox underneath. A tall chimney carried away the smoke and hot gases, and thus created a draft over the fire. Cabins and berths occupied the middle deck. The vessel could carry seventy-five passengers.

Although constructed at Pittsburgh—where the only inland facilities for boat and engine building were located—Fulton and his financial backer, Robert Livingston, never intended this steamboat to operate on the Ohio. They had in mind the deep-water Mississippi between New Orleans and Natchez. To make that point clear, she was christened *New Orleans*. Only fifteen hundred miles of uncharted river stood in their way. For that reason Fulton and Livingston had sent their junior partner down the Ohio and Mississippi in a flatboat to survey the difficulties. He was Nicholas Roosevelt, and he would captain the *New Orleans*.

The voyage began on October 20, 1811, with fifteen people on board, including Roosevelt's pregnant wife. Along the way they endured low water, a fire, an Indian attack, and the New Madrid Earthquake—and witnessed the birth of the Roosevelts' son and the wedding of the boat's engineer and chambermaid. All in all it was a rather eventful ten-week voyage and a fitting introduction to the robust days of river steamboating. A transportation revolution began with that trip and it would last the better part of the nineteenth century.

First steamboats at St. Louis

While the revolution may have brought about a change, the change itself was neither immediate nor perfect. Lawsuits over patents dragged on for six years. Fulton and Livingston tried to persuade the territorial government of Missouri to grant them exclusive rights to operate on the waters of the territory, but were turned down. All of this intrigue served only to delay the expansion and development of steamboat navigation. A mere 18 steamboats had been built by 1817—the year the first steamer reached St. Louis. These early boats were dangerous, unreliable, and inefficient. (The same statement would hold true for the entire steamboating era.) In fact, they often were more trouble than they were worth.

The first steamer to reach St. Louis was the *Zebulon Pike,* a rickety affair with a low-pressure engine, walking beam apparatus, and a single smokestack. The crew had found it necessary to use poles to augment the puny effort of the engine on the voyage from Louisville, Kentucky, to St. Louis. Nevertheless the *Pike* was considered an unqualified success. Although her captain, Jacob Reed, wasn't about to embarrass himself by giving excursion rides in front of the city—and possibly breaking down for all to see, he did permit tours of his boat while she stood at the wharf. Admission was one dollar and there were plenty of takers. A *steam*-boat was something to see. A year after the *Pike's* brief visit, another boat, the *St. Louis,* visited her namesake city. This one gave rides up to the mouth of the Missouri where her passengers contemplated that wild stream and dared wonder if a steamer might successfully attempt a passage. But no, not yet; it would be still another year before any steamboat captain felt confident enough in his vessel to head her west into that semi-solid morass nicknamed the Big Muddy.

First steamboat on the Missouri

It was May, 1819, when the first steamer went up the Missouri. Captain John Nelson had accepted a charter paid for by St. Louis merchants and civic leaders to take his boat, the *Independence,* up

the Missouri River to the vicinity of the Chariton River. The cargo
was flour, whiskey, sugar, and iron, and a passenger list of several
St. Louis notables. It took thirteen days to make the 150-mile
trip—keelboats had done better—but on May 28, 1819, the
Independence puffed up to the landing at Franklin, in the future
Howard County, Missouri, and the celebration began. And a
splendid celebration it was, to be sure. The town of Franklin hosted a grand banquet for the officers and passengers of the
Independence featuring seven hours of food, drinks, and speeches.
A toast followed every speech, and the toasts, according to one par-
ticipant, were of "a stronger beverage" than river water. The chron-
icler of this event lists twenty-three toasts raised and consumed
during the affair—though his count might have been impaired
toward the end.

    The first toast was to the Missouri River: "Its last wave will roll
the abundant tribute of our region to the Mexican gulf, in reference
to the auspices of this day." The next toast went to the memory of
Robert Fulton, inventor of the steamboat; then to Benjamin
Franklin, who never saw a steamboat nor the Missouri River, but the
town had been named for him so why not drink to him; then to
Captain Nelson: "The imaginary dangers of the Missouri vanished
before his enterprising genius."

    After four rounds of good cheer the imaginary dangers of the
Missouri indeed had vanished before the eyes of several of the
worthy celebrators. By the twelfth round the toastmasters had
steered off course and raised their glasses to such topics as "the
purchase of the Floridas—a hard bargain," and other nebulous
subjects. Captain Nelson managed to get to his feet and exclaim:
"I will ever bear in grateful remembrance the liberality and hospi-
tality of the citizens of Franklin." His sentiments came from the
heart, and later were sealed by a powerful throbbing in the head.

The warm, fuzzy recollection of that banquet left the citizens of Franklin thirsting for more, so much so that when the second steamboat reached them, two months later, the celebrations were started anew.

The Yellowstone Expedition and the Western Engineer

The second steamer on the Missouri was the *Western Engineer*. It was part of a grand adventure conceived by the government to send an army and an assortment of scientists up the Missouri to the Yellowstone River. The army was meant to impress the Indians and offset the influence of the meddling British in that quarter. The scientists went along to examine and catalog the plant and animal life of the West. So much importance was placed on this expedition that steamboats, rather than keelboats, were designated to support the movement. This was a great mistake, for steamboats were yet too primitive to tackle the greater length of the Missouri. And as so often was the case, the contract to provide five of the six steamers went to an unscrupulous schemer, James Johnson. Having relied on political cronies, Johnson managed to get the contract at an inflated price and without competition. His boats, the *Thomas Jefferson, Expedition, R.M. Johnson, J. C. Calhoun,* and *Exchange,* were all substandard. A young man from Kentucky, William D. Hubbell, was hired as a clerk on the *R.M. Johnson.* He knew nothing of the backhanded dealing of his employer; he simply had wanted to take part in the westward adventure. Hubbell left Louisville on the *Johnson* in April, 1819. The boat was loaded with army supplies. Many years later he recounted what he remembered of the Yellowstone Expedition:

Our boat had an additional boiler put up and we were much annoyed by the want of a full supply of water when we came to start, but we arrived at St. Louis about the last of April or the first part of May and entered the Missouri in May . . . .

The troops did not arrive and we built a camp opposite the mouth of the Missouri River in Illinois. While detained waiting for the troops, I was given the command of the *Johnson* and made several trips to the mouth of the Ohio, after supplies that had been brought to the mouth in flatboats, which I successfully accomplished and got all back safe.

In the meantime the steamboat *J.C. Calhoun*, [which] was to have been one of the boats to accompany the expedition, [and] had left Louisville to join us, had not arrived or had not been heard from. I was started with one man to go down the river in a canoe to meet her and find out the cause of delay. I started and found her at Cape Girardeau with a hole burnt in her boiler. Of course, nothing could be done with her and I hired a man to take me and my man to Ste. Genevieve, then hired another man to take us to St. Louis, where we arrived about July 1, and joined my boat, the *Johnson,* the next day.

The troops finally got to the old fort, Bellefontaine, about five miles above the mouth of the Missouri River, and the day was finally reached by general order to start from the fort of Bellefontaine . . . for the mouth of the Yellowstone River. At 12 o'clock meridian the signal gun was fired and we began to move in military array. We went along very slowly—the keelboats as well as the steamers. In an hour or two we got into confusion, and hardly got out of sight of the starting place and ran aground, and we did not get all off until the next day, when we arrived at St. Charles, . . . making only 25 miles.

Colonel [Henry] Atkinson then issued an order for each of the boats to act for itself, and they could proceed to act for themselves without waiting for one another. Our boat, *Johnson,* proceeded, but we did not get as far as Cote Sans Dessein when we burnt a hole in the boiler, and had to repair it before we could go on. We were detained 12 days. When we got started again, we were aground every day. Frequently, at nights, we could look back and see the place we started from in the morning. Nobody on our boat had ever run the river before, and we had to feel our way the best we could. However, we got along the best and when we came to a bar that had not sufficient water, we generally ran out a cable to fasten to a log or a tree on shore, and by keeping the boat's bow upstream we would work our way over it, and thus we progressed from day to day until we arrived at Fort Osage, a day or two after the troops that had proceeded us.

The *Western Engineer* had left St. Louis on June 9, 1819, and had stayed well ahead of the boats carrying the military supplies—even allowing for a weeklong celebratory stop at Franklin. The *Western Engineer* was an excellent craft for its time, and unlike the others it was a sternwheeler. But she differed from the others in more than just the wheel arrangement. A letter from an eyewitness relates:

> The bow of this vessel exhibits the form of a huge serpent, black and scaly, rising out of the water from under the boat, his head as high as the deck, darted forward, his mouth open, vomiting smoke, and apparently carrying the boat on his back. From under the boat at its stern issues a stream of foaming water, dashing violently along. All the machinery is hid. Three small brass field pieces [i.e.—cannon] mounted on wheel carriages stand on the deck. The boat is ascending the rapid stream at the rate of three miles an hour. Neither wind nor human hands are seen to help her, and, to the eye of ignorance, the illusion is complete, that a monster of the deep carries her on his back, smoking with fatigue, and lashing the waves with violent exertion. Her equipments are at once calculated to attract and to awe the savages. Objects pleasing and terrifying are at once placed before him—artillery, the flag of the Republic, portraits of the white man and the Indian shaking hands, the calumet of peace, a sword, then the apparent monster with a painted vessel on his back, the sides gaping with portholes and bristling with guns. Taken altogether, and without intelligence of her composition and design, it would require a daring savage to approach and accost her with Hamlet's speech: "Be thou a spirit of health or goblin damned . . . ?"

The *Western Engineer* reached Fort Osage on August 1st, and passed the future site of Fort Leavenworth on the 18th. After a week's layover in the vicinity, she arrived at Fort Lisa, five miles below Council Bluffs, on the 17th of September. This was far short of the Yellowstone, but since the military supply boats were far behind, the expedition leaders decided to make winter quarters here. Hubbell and the *Johnson* were still at Fort Osage, a long 470 miles below. The disparity was about to grow worse; shortly after the *Johnson* left Fort Osage she burst her cylinder head and was totally disabled. At that early day there were no foundries west of Louisville, and Louisville was more than five hundred miles from Fort Osage. The officers of the boat agreed that their only choice was to fetch another cylinder head. The engineer removed the engine, for there were no such things as blueprints nor duplicate parts, and with his assistants he carried the burdensome thing to the fort and arranged to send it and himself to Louisville by keelboat. He would make it back in four months.

With winter coming on, and funds for the expedition running low, clerk Hubbell was ordered to lead the crewmen back to Louisville where they would be furloughed for the season. A keelboat took them as far as St. Louis, but they walked the remaining two hundred and fifty miles through regions infested with cutthroats and robbers. They arrived home, wrote Hubbell, "the sorest and tiredest set of men I ever saw." In February, 1820, Hubbell and crew returned to the *Johnson,* to await the spring thaw and the return of their boat's engine.

By April the engine, with its new cylinder head, had been installed, and the Missouri River had risen enough to resume navigation. But the winter months had taken their toll on the *Johnson's* hull. The awkward craft now seemed inclined to shake herself apart. The officers decided to take her back to St. Louis, in company with her sister steamer, the *Expedition,* to see if anything could be done to refit her. The boats arrived in St. Louis a few weeks later, and although no one there knew very much about steamboats, it was certain to those who examined her that the *Johnson* would not survive another ascent of the unforgiving Missouri. She would be sent instead to Louisville and dismantled. Will Hubbell transferred to the *Expedition,* a better boat, and helped load her with supplies for the small army that was marching its way farther upriver. Hubbell resumes his tale:

We loaded the *Expedition* for [Council] Bluffs and left St. Louis, I think in May, and as we had learned something of the river by experience we got along a good deal better and successfully made the trip up with the steamboat to the Bluffs. Got there in July. It was determined to let the boat stay at the Bluffs, under the protection of the fort, and I remained in charge of her with two men under me and we were to bring her out in the spring.

That summer representatives from all the various tribes, from the Missouri to the Rocky Mountains, were assembled at the Bluffs to hold treaties with the agent, Colonel John O'Fallon of St. Louis. I was much amused one day by an Indian coming on board and seeing himself in a large mirror in the cabin; he ran off and soon brought, I suppose, 100 or more with him to look at the wonderful sight. After they had crowded in as many as could see, they ludicrously broke out into a loud and boisterous laugh, which was truly funny. The glass attracted more sightseeing than anything at the Bluffs. I noticed an Indian one day, sitting on the bank of the river, earnestly looking at the boat, when all at once he made a dive, as if to go under the boat, which really was his object, but he went the whole length of the boat and came up at the stern awfully bruised and scratched.

I was taken sick with chills and fever and at last got so low that the surgeon of the boat told me that the only possible chance to save my life was to leave there and try and get back home. As a keelboat was going down to St. Louis, and several of the officers were going home on furlough, I left the boat in charge of Major Doughterty and came down. At St. Louis we hired a hack and came through to Louisville, four of us, and I got home at last, nearer dead than alive.

In one year the steamboats of the expedition had ascended only 860 miles to Council Bluffs, and that would end it. There were still another eight hundred miles of hazardous channel ahead before reaching the Yellowstone River, and the boats were not up to the task—not even the *Western Engineer.* Congress cancelled further funding of the venture.

"I can truly say," wrote Hubbell, "that the whole matter of the steamboats was as complete a failure as could have been possible, the boats being totally unfit for the trip." It took another eleven years for any steamboat to complete the trek. The Yellowstone

Expedition of 1819-20 had proven two things: first, that the Missouri was one tough river to climb; and, second, that steamboats needed a lot of improvement.

Early designs

Much of the improvement came in the person of Henry M. Shreve. A competitor of the Fulton-Livingston concern, Shreve understood that Western River steamboats would require a design much different from Hudson River or coastal steamers. With his partner, Daniel French, Shreve turned out a steamer in 1813, and another in 1814. Essentially they were experimental prototypes. Then, in 1816, Shreve conceived a new boat that he named *Washington*. The *Washington* slid off the ways with a flatter bottom and with its machinery on the main deck instead of in the hold. Shreve eliminated the heavy walking beam apparatus and replaced it with engines mounted horizontally. The rods, or pitmans, now connected the engine directly with the paddlewheel crank. With these basic innovations in place, all other problems could be worked out in time.

First-generation Missouri River boats generally measured 100 to 130 feet in length with 20- to 30-foot beams. They would draw three to five feet of water. Their upstream progress was no more than six miles per hour. Joseph Brown, a young man living in St. Louis at the time, later put down on paper what he could remember of those early-day steamboats:

> They had but one engine . . . . The boats themselves, and particularly those for the upper rivers, were small, sometimes made like a flatboat, with broad bow and stern, and a sternwheel. There was nothing above the boiler deck but the pilothouse and the chimneys, or rather one chimney, for they had cylinder boilers: that is, there were no flues in the boilers. Having but one engine, the shaft ran clean across the boat, and

when at a landing the engine had to run the pump to supply the boilers with water, the wheels had to be uncoupled to let the engine work . . . . The doctor engine had not been invented, and I do not doubt that many explosions occurred for the lack of it.

The cabin was a very primitive affair. It was on the lower deck, back of the shaft, in the after part of the boat. There were no staterooms then, but, like a canal boat, there were curtains in front of the berths. It was quite common to see a bowsprit sticking out in front of the boat, such as are used on ships, but, being useless, they were soon dispensed with. Stages had not been invented then. Two or three planks were used, and, if need be, tied together. Whistles were unknown, but bells were rung, and the captains were very proud of a big bell.

There were no regular packets then. I have known boats to have steam up for a week, telling people and shippers the boat was going in an hour, and even have their planks taken in, all but one, and then launch their planks out again. All this was done to decoy people on board. The clanging of bells, the hurrah of agents, and the pulling and hauling of cabmen and runners were most confusing, more particularly to unsophisticated emigrants. There was no fixed price for anything; it was all a matter of bargain, and very often great deception was practiced.

The engines being small and very imperfect in those days, the boats were very slow. I have known some of the boats in the case of a sudden rise in the river and consequent strong current, to be unable to stem it at the old waterworks plant, which was at the foot of Carr Street. They would have to go over to the other side of the river and fight it out there, sometimes for hours, in sight of the city.

Early accommodations

Passenger accommodations underwent an evolutionary process. The first boats were no grand hotels. Take, for example, this description from a not-too-pleased traveler of an early day:

> The cabin was on the lower deck, immediately abaft the boilers, with a small partition at the stern set apart for the females. There were no staterooms, no wash room, nor even a social hall; and therefore, on the guard—within two inches of the level of the river, and about two feet wide, with nothing to prevent your falling overboard if your foot slipped,...you made your toilet, with a good chunk of yellow soap on a

stool, to which two tin basins were chained, and alongside a barrel of water. The cabin contained thirty-two berths. In the daytime these were piled up with the surplus mattresses and blankets which, at night, were spread close together on the floor, and under and on the dining tables, for so many of the passengers as were fortunate enough to have precedence even in this luxury, after the berths were disposed of. The remainder of the party sat up, drinking, smoking, playing cards, or grumbling at not being able to find a single horizontal space, under cover, large enough to stretch their weary limbs on . . . .

The upper level of this last-described steamer simply may have been an open promenade deck, with canvas awnings for shade, and above which the pilothouse and smokestacks protruded. In short, there was much wasted space. It hit upon someone, whose name was long forgotten, to move the cabins to the upper deck so as to leave the main deck open for more freight and machinery. The following description, written by a passenger in November, 1832, details how far steamboat architecture had come in the span of a few short years:

> The boilers, which are cylindrical, and vary from four to double that number, are placed forward on the main deck, and behind them the machinery is arranged towards the center of the vessel, enclosed between the huge paddle-boxes and a row of offices on either side.
> Sometimes a ladies' cabin is constructed on the same deck, in the stern of the boat; but, more generally, this part is given up to the so-called deck passengers, and the whole range of superior cabins is built upon an upper deck, extending from the stern over that part of the vessel where the boilers are situated, the portion most in advance being called the boiler deck. Through the latter, the great chimney pipes conducting the smoke from the fires below ascend, and as the range of cabins do not extend quite so far, the open space and view afforded by it renders it a favorite lounge.
> Of the disposition of the cabins little need be said. The ladies' apartment is aft, and opens with sliding doors and curtains into the main, or gentleman's cabin, which is frequently fifty or sixty feet in length. Both are furnished with handsome tiers of upper and lower berths, canopied with ample chintz or moreen curtains, and the former cabin is frequently fitted up with staterooms. A gallery runs round the whole exterior. Between the

forward end of the great cabin and the boiler deck, ten or fifteen feet of the deck is ordinarily occupied by a bar, washing room, [and] captain's and stewards' offices, ranged on either side of an anti-chamber.

Cabin passage

Cabin passage entitled the traveler to a stateroom and meals in the main cabin. The meals were varied and the food was plentiful. Stewards and chambermaids kept things tidy. Details of the cabin and staterooms caught the eye of Joseph Cowell in 1844. Cowell traveled a great deal as an actor, author, and painter, and has this to say about steamboat interiors:

> The saloon, or principal chamber, extends nearly the whole length of the boat, on the upper deck,…terminating forward with large glazed doors opening on a covered space called the boiler deck, and aft by the ladies cabin, with which it communicates by folding doors, which are generally left open in warm weather, in the daytime. The whole is lighted from above by a continuous skylight, round the side of a long oval, which looks as if it had been cut out from the ceiling, and lifted some two feet above it perpendicularly, and there supported by framed glass. On either side of this carpeted and splendidly furnished apartment are ranged the staterooms, the doors ornamented with Venetian or cut-glass windows, and assisting, by their long line of perspective, the general effect. These small chambers usually contain two berths, never more, which always look as if you were the first person who had ever slept in them— with curtains, mosquito-bars, toilet stands, drawers, chairs, carpets, and all the elegant necessaries of a cozy bedroom. In many of the larger boats double staterooms are provided for families, and young married people who are afraid to sleep by themselves, with four-post bedsteads.

Deck passage

With the cabin and staterooms placed above on the boiler deck, the first-class passengers enjoyed a splendid isolation from the noise and odor of the main deck. A professional travel writer of the period noted that the main deck usually was crowded with freight, cargo, machinery, and livestock. He overlooked one other commodity below, and perhaps he meant to, for in the class-conscious Victorian times one did not write of the impoverished and destitute. Down there on the main deck rode dozens—even hundreds—of poor, wretched individuals and families, mostly immigrants, who were moving inland in search of their ideal, whatever and wherever that might be. On ocean vessels they called it steerage class, on the river it was deck passage; in either instance it could be a hellish experience, especially for a family with small children.

Deck passage averaged half the cost of cabin fare; it entitled the rider to basic transportation between two points, and little else. Deck passengers were not allowed access to the staterooms or main cabin, they had to provide their own bedding, they paid extra for meals or else brought their own, and they were required to yield space to regular freight. They huddled amongst filth and noise, with no privacy and only minimal shelter from the elements. Some boats required deck passengers to assist in wooding and firing. The deck crews frequently abused them for getting in the way, and stole from them, and even left them stranded at woodyards or freight landings. A boat that carried eighty cabin passengers might carry 300 deck passengers, and these nameless souls were several times more likely than their more fortunate brethren upstairs to be killed in an explosion or sinking.

Captains seldom did anything to alleviate the hardships of deck passage. To the contrary, they frequently overloaded their boats with "deckers" to offset losses in cabin passage revenue. Being mostly immigrants, the deckers usually did not complain of their treatment to authorities for fear of drawing too much attention to themselves. Ironically, the law favored them in many instances. According to federal statutes, a minimum of fifteen square feet of deck space was allotted to each deck passenger. The space had to be "clear of obstruction, and easy of access." Furthermore, the area was to be in a "suitably enclosed deck-room, which shall be properly warmed in cool weather, and properly vented at all times." Passengers aboard the *Helen McGregor* on the Mississippi in 1832 probably had about the right amount of room, and no one could argue that it was not properly ventilated. But whether or not it was adequate, or even humane, should be judged only after reading this eyewitness experience:

> It was night, and in December, raining and making believe to snow, when I arrived on board. She was crowded with passengers: perhaps a hundred in the cabin, and at least that number upon deck; for at that time the steerage occupied the space now allotted to the saloon, and was filled to overflowing with men, women, and children, chiefly Irish and German laborers, with their families, in dirty dishabille. This man-pen was furnished with a stove, for warmth and domestic cooking, and two large, empty shelves, one above the other, all round, boarded up outside about four feet high. These served for sleeping places for those who had bedding, or those who were obliged to plank it; the remaining space above these roosts was only protected from the weather by tattered canvas curtains between the pillars which supported the hurricane deck, alias the roof, which was spread over with a multitude of cabbages, making sauerkraut of themselves as fast as possible, and at least fifty coops of fighting-cocks, each in a separate apartment, with a hole in the front for his head to come through; and their continual notes of defiance, mixed up with the squalling and squeaking of women and children, and the boisterous mirth or vehement quarreling of the men, in all kinds of languages, altogether kicked up a rumpus that drowned even the noise of the engine, which was only separated from the cabin by a thin partition.

Visual appeal

By the mid-1840s Western River steamboats had assumed the classic triple deck layout that would see them through to the end of the era. They were marvelous works of carpenter gothic; each new boat heralded the latest advances in function and style. Eventually steamboat motif outclassed anything seen on shore. Many residents along the river looked upon steamboats as the most beautiful of all structures; little wonder they coined the phrase "elegant as a steamboat." And they not only were elegant, but large and substantially built

Steamboats came in all colors—of white—but an occasional spray of pigment and an accent of tone offered pleasant contrast to the bright, glaring superstructure. Decks and roofs often were darkened with shades of blue. Typically a red stripe, painted on a white hull, ran parallel to the waterline; a few boats sported red or green hulls. The most aesthetically pleasing opportunity for adding color to the boats' exteriors came in the design and trim of paddlewheel housings. Here, bold and husky letters, with bright-colored shadowing, visually shouted the boat's name to all that came in view. Sometimes the title of the packet company or the points of destination would appear in an arc along the upper edge of the housings, and paintings frequently graced the wheelhouse sides. These works of commercial art ranged from simple sunburst patterns to intricate murals that in some manner depicted the name of the boat.

Color and distinction also were added through the gaudy display of banners and flags. Besides the jackstaff on the bow and the verge-staff on the stern, there were additional flagstaffs near the wheel-houses. The national colors flew at the verge; from the other staffs waved brightly trimmed pennants heralding the name of the boat and the principal cities it served. Etiquette suggested that the city or person for whom the boat was named should donate the banners when the steamer made her first port call. It was all very flashy, all very colorful, and of course, all intended to attract business.

Paddlewheel arrangements

The most distinctive external features of riverboats were the paddlewheels. During the steamboat era, ocean vessels evolved from sails to paddlewheels to screw propellers, while riverboats retained the paddle throughout. There was a reason for this. Steam engines of the mid-nineteenth century were capable of producing a great deal of power, but they were unable to turn high revolutions. A slow-turning propeller had to be at least seven or eight feet in diameter to produce the necessary thrust for an average steamboat, and the Western Rivers frequently were not that deep. Furthermore, experimentation on small vessels with correspondingly smaller propellers pointed out the vulnerability of the blades to driftwood and other debris. The same experiments showed that sand in the water rapidly cut away at the underwater shaft bearings.

STERNWHEELER *DACOTAH*. Launched in 1879, the 252-foot long *Dacotah* was one of the last and largest Missouri River packets. She made seven trips to Fort Benton and set a record for freight tonnage between Kansas City and St. Louis with a load of wheat and miscellaneous cargo estimated at 900 tons. She was dismantled in 1893.
(PHOTO COURTESY MURPHY LIBRARY, UNIVERSITY OF WISCONSIN-LA CROSSE.)

In every way, paddlewheels were better suited to the river. No matter how large their diameter, they extended only two to three feet below the waterline, and they could be adjusted for less. The individual paddles—called buckets—struck the water at the rate of three to four hundred per minute even though the wheel itself was turning at a mere twelve or fifteen revolutions. The buckets were made of wood, and most boats carried spares; if broken by a floating log, buckets could be replaced with minimal trouble. And paddlewheel bearings were located high above the water where normal friction was the only enemy.

Paddlewheels could be mounted at the sides, at the stern, or inboard amidships. This latter arrangement was confined to ferryboats where it was convenient to have a double-ended vessel with plenty of deck space. Otherwise, mid-ship, or centerwheel, steamers lacked commercial speed due to the inherent disadvantages of their design.

Sidewheelers were best adapted to mercantile use. Unlike the single engine and common shaft arrangement of the very earliest models, later sidewheelers utilized independent wheels with two separate engines. In a difficult navigational situation, one wheel could be set ahead, with the other turning in reverse, and the boat would twist around like a pinwheel. They also handled better in tricky winds and currents. But sidewheelers had disadvantages, as well. The paddles were unprotected by the hull and therefore subject to damage by floating logs; vibration was at times excessive; the boats were heavier and more expensive to build than sternwheelers of similar dimensions; and the peculiar fluid mechanics of sidewheel propulsion sometimes rendered the rudder ineffective.

Sternwheel boats were considered the most powerful of the three types, and the hull protected the wheel from most floating hazards. For a long time in their evolution, sternwheelers

were plagued with soft rudder response that made them difficult to manage in high winds and strong currents. Placing additional rudders on the transom did little to overcome this. Then,
in the 1870s, the "balance rudder" came into general use on
sternwheelers. This rudder featured an enlarged surface area,
about half of which extended in front of the rudder post. The
remarkable handling improvement that resulted from this
innovation made sternwheelers the vessel of preference late in
the steamboat era.

Engines

Engine types also varied from boat to boat, but here the variations
were relatively minor. The common differences were piston size,
length of stroke, and arrangement of valve mechanisms. The one
fundamental distinction in power plants came in the use of high-
pressure versus low-pressure engines. The low-pressure engine, as
seen on the *New Orleans* and occasionally revived on larger vessels
throughout the steamboat era, derived much of its power from a
condenser. Water jets within the condenser cooled the steam as it
exhausted from the piston cylinder, and this created a partial vacuum. Aided by this vacuum, the steam on the expansion side of
the stroke entered the cylinder at a pressure only moderately higher than the outside atmosphere.

   Boiler explosions on low-pressure boats were rare, and the traveling public knew this, but low-pressure engines, like screw propellers, were ill suited to conditions on the Western Rivers. The
condensing apparatus was complicated, heavy, and brittle. Repair
facilities for machinery of that kind were nonexistent in most river
cities. Low-pressure engines were not as powerful, and could not
respond as quickly to sudden throttle applications; on a turbid

river pilots needed sure and immediate response from the engines to get the boat out of trouble. Also, boilers that generated low-pressure were more apt to clog with mud. Boiler water was continually pumped in from the river. A sump device known as the mud drum was supposed to collect sediment—and did to a point, but it was an imperfect device. With high-pressure boilers much of the mud remaining in the boiler blew out harmlessly through the safety valve. One passenger, who probably was expressing typical sentiments of his day, acknowledged the "great danger" of high-pressure engines, but he felt that the danger came from "incompetent and careless persons" who attended them. After questioning engineers and captains, this passenger of 1832 admitted that "much might be said in favor of high-pressure engines."

Wooding up

As a rule, passengers did not comprehend the mechanical workings of the boat; most stayed away from the engine and boiler spaces where a disapproving stare and occasional hard comment from an oily engineer let them know they were not welcome. The typical passenger knew only that the boat required wood—lots of it—to keep the engines going. Small entrepreneurs who operated wood-yards along the riverbanks of the Lower Missouri fulfilled this need. "Wooding up" was often the highlight of the day on an otherwise dull stretch of river. A stop for wooding might take up to an hour and usually was performed twice a day. Passengers could go ashore to escape the confinement of the boat during a wooding stop, though often they would line the railings to watch the spectacle. All the deckhands, roustabouts, and even deck passengers who had purchased their ride for reduced fare, turned to for the heavy work of loading by hand. Very often an "exciting physical contest" would ensue to determine who could carry the largest pile, and the passengers would cheer for their favorites. One traveler wrote that during this rush to get the wood aboard, the mate of the boat "divided his time between exhortations of 'Oh, bring them shavings along! Don't go to sleep at this frolic,' and by swearing of such monstrous proportions, that even very good men are puzzled to decide whether he is really profane or simply ridiculous." Although the passenger who observed and recorded this episode was writing of a trip on the Mississippi River, the same scene was played out daily all along the Lower Missouri. The writer added:

> It is a singular fact that when a steamer hails a woodyard no direct answer to any question is ever obtained. We believe there has been no exception to this rule even in the memory of the oldest steamboat captain on the river. The steamer is desirous of getting "ash wood," providing it is "seasoned." The captain, as his boat approaches the shore, places his hands to his mouth, and forming them into a tube, calls out, "What kind of wood is that?"
>
> The reply comes back, "Cord wood."
>
> The captain, still in pursuit of information under difficulties, and desirous of learning if the fuel be dry and fit for his purpose, bawls out: "How long has it been cut?"
>
> "Four feet," is the prompt response.
>
> The captain, exceedingly vexed, next inquires, "What do you sell it for?"
>
> "Cash," returns the chopper, replacing the corn cob pipe in his mouth, and smiling benignly on his pile.
>
> Woodyards are apparently infested with mosquitoes—we say apparently infested. Such is the impression of all accidental sojourners; but it is a strange delusion, for though one may think that they fill the air, inflame the face and hands, and if of the Arkansas species, penetrate the flesh through the thickest boots, still upon inquiring of any permanent resident if mosquitoes are numerous, the invariable answer is: "Mosquitoes—no! Not about here. But a little way down the river they are awful—*thar* they torment alligators to death, and sting mules right through their hoofs!"

I will only remind you that steam navigation on the Missouri is one of the most dangerous things a man can undertake. I fear the sea, but all the storms and other unpleasant things I have experienced in four different ocean voyages did not inspire me with so much terror as the navigation of the somber, treacherous, muddy Missouri.

FATHER PIERRE-JEAN DESMET

2

The Fickle River

Missouri River Mileage

A Comparison of Modern-Day River Mileage to Distances Reported in 1846 by the St. Joseph Gazette

Measured from the St. Louis Wharf

Location	1846	Present-day
Mouth of the Missouri	20	15
St. Charles	45	43
Washington	89	83
Hermann	117	113
Mouth of the Gasconade	125	104
Cote Sans Dessein	157	147*
Mouth of the Osage	159	145*
Jefferson City	169	158
Rocheport	210	201
Boonville	222	212
Mouth of the Lamine	230	217
Arrow Rock	238	226
Glasgow	253	241
Mouth of the Chariton	254	242
Brunswick	284	269#
Mouth of the Grand	285	265#
Lexington	351	332
Wellington	359	338
Camden	368	+
Napoleon	376	344
Fort Osage (Sibley)	384	352
Mouth of the Little Blue	392	354
Blue Mills Landing	404	+
Liberty	410	+
Wayne City (Independence)	415	369
Mouth of the Big Blue	418	372
Randolph	423	375
Westport Landing (Kansas City)	429	381
Mouth of the Kansas	431	382
Fort Leavenworth	467	412
Weston	475	417
St. Joseph	544	463
Council Bluffs (Omaha)	863	631

* The mouth of the Osage River is now 4 miles east of its 1846 location.

Due to a cutoff Brunswick now fronts Grand River, 4 miles above the Missouri. Grand River follows the old Missouri bed and empties into the Missouri 5 miles below its 1846 mouth.

+ No longer on the river due to cutoffs.

The nature of the river

The Missouri is the longest river in North America. It measures over 2,300 miles. That is at present-day. In 1861 the U.S. Army Topographical Engineers determined the length of the Missouri to be 2,824 miles. This discrepancy of some 500 miles can be explained by the river's centuries-old habit of straightening itself out, and thus shortening its length. During the steamboat era the Missouri River was navigable, in season, from its mouth, twenty miles above St. Louis, to Fort Benton, Montana, falling 2,464 feet in 2,644 miles—a slope of 11 inches per mile. This was the average slope. In fact, the Missouri did not fall in a straight line, but descended more in the shape of a parabola: steeper on the upper river, flatter on the lower.

The Missouri River flowed through an alluvial plain. This fine sediment of the millenniums offered little resistance to the swift current, especially during floods; nevertheless, the accumulation of debris and the variations of soil permeability deflected the stream left and right and set off an imbalance of hydraulic pressure which the river continually attempted to equalize. The result was an unending succession of loops and bends.

And wherever the river started a bend it seemed disinclined to leave it alone; it expended its energy to make the bend larger and longer. By throwing the considerable power of its moving water against the outer shore, the river would eat away at a bank and chisel a great, arching curve through what had been field and forest only days before. This was an immutable law of the river and a continual process occurring at many places at the same time. These natural realignments, caused by unpredictable random force, could play havoc with property lines and real estate values. Special laws were placed on the books just to cover the contingencies. Consider, for example, this story of the Missouri River from the 1890s:

> It is a perpetual dissatisfaction with its bed that is the greatest peculiarity of the Missouri. It is harder to suit in the matter of beds than a traveling man. Time after time it has gotten out of its bed in the middle of the night, with no apparent provocation, and has hunted up a new bed, all littered with forests, cornfields, brick houses, railroad ties, and telegraph poles. It has flopped into this prickly mess with a gurgle of content and has flowed along placidly, for years, gradually assimilating the foreign substances and wearing down the bumps in its alluvial mattress. Then it has suddenly taken a fancy to its old bed, which by this time has been filled with suburban architecture, and back it has gone with a whoop and a rush, as happy as if it had really found something worthwhile.
>
> These facts lead us naturally to the subject of the Missouri's appetite. It is the hungriest river ever created. It is eating all the time—eating yellow clay banks and cornfields, eighty acres at a mouthful; winding up its banquet with a truck garden and picking its teeth with the timbers of a big red barn. Its yearly menu is ten thousand acres of good rich farming land, several miles of railroad, a few hundred houses, a forest or two, and uncounted miles of sandbars. Throw a man into the Missouri and he will not often drown. It is more likely that he will break his leg.
>
> On the Iowa side of the river, a few miles away [from Council Bluffs,] the Burlington Railroad runs up the valley. Years ago the river began to show a liking for the railroad. It edged up closer and closer and finally swallowed a few rods of it. The company took the hint and moved back half a mile. The river followed after, like an affectionate Newfoundland pup.
>
> The company attempted dissuasionary measures. It carted a hundred carloads of stone to the river bank and dropped them in. The river

smacked its lips and swallowed the stone along with another acre of land for good measure. A thousand loads were dumped in. Not a trace of stone could be found the next day. Then the railroad company drove immense piles deep into the ground and anchored them with steel chains, big enough to hold a battleship in leash. The river didn't waste time with the bulwark, but just swallowed the whole field in which it was located and leaped joyfully on toward the railroad tracks.

Then the railroad company gave up and moved back among the foothills. After this was done the Missouri moved, too. It went over to the other side of the valley, leaving another of its celebrated loops which today is beautiful Lake Manawa, one of the finest pleasure spots in the Central West.

Quite naturally this makes life along the Missouri a bit uncertain. Ask the citizen of a Missouri River town on which side of the river he lives, and he will look worried and will say, "On the east side when I came away." Then he will go home and look the matter up and, like as not, will find the river on the other side of his humble home and a government steamboat pulling snags out of his erstwhile cabbage patch.

It makes farming as fascinating as gambling, too. You never know whether you are going to harvest corn or catfish. The farmer may go blithely forth of a morning with a twine binder to cut his wheat, only to come back at noon for a trot-line—his wheat having gone down the river the night before.

This sort of thing makes the Missouri Valley farmer philosophical in the extreme. The river may take away half his farm this year, but he feels sure that next year it will give him the whole farm of the fellow above him. But he must not be too certain. At this point the law steps in and does a more remarkable thing than the river itself may hope to accomplish. It decrees that so long as there is a single yard of an owner's land left—nay, even so long as there is a strip wide enough to balance a calf upon, he is entitled to all the land that the river may deposit in front of it. But when that last yard is eaten up, even though the river may repent and replace the farm in as good order as when it took it, the land belongs to the owner of the land behind it. There is no way of getting around this decision. All the despoiled owner can do is to buy the farm in back of his erstwhile farm and wait patiently for the river to eat up his land. Then, if it recedes, he may not only get his farm back but the one between his old one and his new one and possibly a few more for good measure. Roulette is child's play compared with it.

This thing happened in Kansas City not many years ago. A party of men owned a strip of land along the Missouri River bank. It was not handsome land, but it was valuable for factory purposes. They were offered portly prices for it, but held on.

One day they noticed that the strip was getting emaciated. They held a hurried diagnosis with a surveyor's tape and found that half of it had wasted away. The next year half of the remainder had gone.

The men wanted to sell then, but the market seemed remarkably sluggish. The next year the river ate so vigorously that only a tiny strip about as wide as a piece of baby ribbon was left. The men were much depressed.

Suddenly the land began to increase. The Missouri had chosen the late manufacturing site to deposit a fine 160-acre farm upon which it had foreclosed up the river. Inside of six months that strip of land contained 200 acres. The men were jubilant, but still they could not sell. They wanted another 100 acres, they said. They strolled along the bank each day and urged the river, in proprietary tones, to build faster.

Then the river changed its mind once more and not only wiped out the extra 100 acres, but the original 100 acres, every foot of it. The next year it built up 500 acres in the same spot, but they all belonged to the men who owned the ground behind the original plot. The acreage has stayed there ever since—that is, up to last reports. For high financing and property juggling, the Missouri makes a crooked lawyer look like a child. I hate to think what it would do for a man if it had a personal friendship for him.

The channel

The deepest part of the river—the channel—was an elusive, ill-defined, narrow ditch that coursed its way back and forth across the river bed. The channel seldom ran down the middle of the river, and any steamboat that got out of the channel, as they were often wont to do, would soon find herself hard aground, or worse.

The channel comprised only a small portion of the river's overall width, and the channel line often disappeared in a given stretch of river to such an extent that even a skilled and experienced steersman could not "read" it. Centrifugal action forced the greater volume of water to the outside of a bend, and there the channel ran deep and wide. But the river, like a serpent, always reversed itself from bend to bend so that the channel moved from one side to the other. The point at which the channel changed over—the crossing—was far and away the least defined and shallowest portion of the river bed. During low water the current in the crossing could decrease to the point that sediment would build up in the form of a reef or bar and effectively block navigation. Only a rise in the water level would remedy the situation.

Sediment

The Missouri River was the champion bank-caving, sediment-carrying, tree-toppling stream of all the Western waterways. It suspended 120 tons of sediment in every million gallons of water, ten times the amount of the Lower Mississippi. The Missouri was the

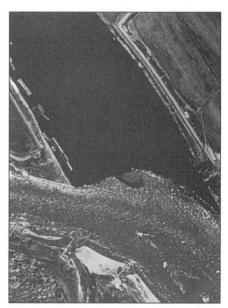

CONFLUENCE OF THE MISSISSIPPI AND MISSOURI RIVERS. The turbulent, silt-laden Missouri (entering from the left) overwhelms the darker waters of the Mississippi. The confluence is 15 miles north of St. Louis—it has worked its way five miles farther down since the days of steam packetboats.
(PHOTO COURTESY U.S. ARMY CORPS OF ENGINEERS.)

muddiest river on the continent and most travelers were moved to comment about it. The eminent journalist Horace Greeley came upon the Missouri at St. Joseph in 1859. After examining the curious liquid, he wrote to his paper in New York: "Its color and consistency are those of thick milk porridge; you could not discern an egg in a glass of it."

The popular adage had it that the Missouri was too thin to cultivate and too thick to drink. But some hearty rivermen did drink it, regularly. The Missouri, it seemed, contained high amounts of volcanic ash. Those who routinely partook of it experienced fewer, well, digestive problems. When a lady from the East, who should have known better, persisted in asking a leathery Missouri River captain why he drank the water, the boatman replied: "'Cause it scours out your bowels, ma'am."

The flood of 1844

The great inundations of the Missouri have occurred approximately every fifty years. Since the beginning of powered navigation, big floods have taken place in 1844, 1903, 1951, and 1993. The 1844 rise was the greatest. It was thought to be the result of concentrated, heavy rainfall over Kansas and Missouri in May and June. A St. Louis newspaper reported "rain and sunshine alternate every day and every hour of the day." The river completely filled its bottomland from St. Joseph to the mouth, and its lower tributaries were equally swelled. The Gasconade River was twenty miles wide where it flowed into the Missouri just above Hermann. The Missouri's brown tide was choked with debris: trees, houses, and bloated livestock raced along with the current and knocked down anything still standing. A handful of steamboats continued their journeys through the floating obstacle course, but not always with success.

The *Mary Tomkins* lost headway near Liberty. The strong current, together with a high wind, sent her tearing out of the channel, crashing through a belt of timber, and sailing through open farmland known as Wakenda Prairie. A passenger on the boat said that the *Tomkins* had bowled over fifty large trees on her wild rampage through the woods. The *Iatan* struck a floating tree with such force that the trunk deflected upward and pierced two upper decks and a stateroom. Boats that escaped damage were hard pressed to find dry wood for their boilers, and nearly all the steamers that continued operating during the flood spent as much time plucking people off housetops and trees as they did running their regular trip.

The flood receded by mid-July, and in its wake there flowed a very different river. The Missouri had realigned itself in many places. Just above Wayne City, for example, the river had cut a sharper bend and in the process had moved the mouth of the Big Blue River about a mile farther down. Over the next few years this change caused the Missouri to shoal up at Wayne City, eventually to the point of building an island in front of the place. This cut off Wayne City landing from the main channel and put it instead behind the island, on a chute. Steamboats could no longer land there except in high river stages. Wayne City was the principal landing site for the town of Independence, located some three miles inland. Independence thrived on its river connections: it literally owed its prosperity to Oregon and California Trail emigrants and Santa Fe traders who used the river to travel from the East. Now that very commerce began to decline, and over the next decade Independence saw its monopoly of westward trade broken by towns higher up on the Missouri, towns that could boast of deep water landings and shorter routes to the West. The speculators at Independence took steps to retain the traffic. They built a wharf of stone at Wayne City, they paved the road to Independence, they

even built a railroad between the landing and the town in 1850—
the first railroad west of the Mississippi—but all for naught. The
great Missouri had ruled against Independence; the town never
again would know the prosperity of its former times.

The flood of 1844 caused other problems. Sand dunes five feet
high covered once-productive fields, and the lower river was a
nightmare to navigate. The bottom presented an uncharted succession of reefs and troughs, the channel scarcely was more than two
feet deep, and logs and snags stuck out of the water like military
abatis. The steamer *Tobacco Plant* had to send her crew ahead in
rowboats to clear debris from the river, and probably she was but
one of several boats that resorted to the measure that season. Only
the passage of time and a redoubled effort by the pilots to learn the
new channel brought river commerce back to a normal gait.

Snags

Travelers of an earlier day looked upon the river with a sense of
reverence; it clearly was one of God's more spectacular creations. It
also was at times a force that knew no bounds—an awesome,
frightening thing not to be taken lightly. Father Pierre-Jean
DeSmet, a Jesuit missionary who traveled extensively, spent several years along the Upper Missouri. His writings were not given to
overstatement, and yet he had this to say about the grim river:

> I will only remind you that steam navigation on the Missouri is one
> of the most dangerous things a man can undertake. I fear the sea, but all
> the storms and other unpleasant things I have experienced in four dif-
> ferent ocean voyages did not inspire me with so much terror as the nav-
> igation of the somber, treacherous, muddy Missouri.

In order to improve their chances against the hazards of the
Missouri, some boats carried iron plating on their bows to reduce

damage from drifting logs, and ice. But when floating tree trunks affixed themselves in the riverbed, even iron plated prows were vulnerable. These snags, with one end buried in the mire and the other slanting upward toward the surface, were the most dreaded of the river's obstructions. John Bradbury saw them when he rode downriver on a keelboat in 1811. He remarked that the riverbanks were heavily forested, and many of the trees fell into the river during periods of high water. He continues:

> As in most instances a large body of earth is attached to the roots of the trees, it sinks that part to the bottom of the river, whilst the upper part, more buoyant, rises to the surface in an inclined posture, generally with the head of the tree pointing down the river. Some of these are firmly fixed and immovable, and are therefore termed planters. Others, although they do not remove from where they are placed, are constantly in motion, the whole tree is sometimes entirely submerged by the pressure of the stream, and carried to a greater depth by its momentum than the stream can maintain. On rising, its momentum in the other direction causes many of its huge limbs to be lifted above the surface of the river. The period of this oscillatory motion is sometimes of several minutes duration. These are the sawyers, and are much more dangerous than the planters, as no care or caution can guard sufficiently against them. The steersman this instant sees all the surface of the river smooth and tranquil, and the next he is struck with horror on seeing just before him the sawyer raising [its] terrific arms, and so near that neither strength nor skill can save him from destruction.

More than once Father DeSmet had seen a certain ominous-looking stretch of river called the Devil's Rake. It was located about a mile above Weston, Missouri, and was dreaded by all the boatmen. DeSmet wrote:

> It has the appearance of a whole forest, swallowed up by the immense river. Gigantic trees stretch their naked and menacing limbs on all sides; you see them thrashing in the water, throwing up foam with a furious hissing sound as they struggle against the rapid torrent.

The Devil's Rake was but one of hundreds of snag infested reaches of the Missouri. As long as trees grew in the floodplain and along the shores, the Missouri River sooner or later would pick them up and carry them until they rotted away or became impaled on bars and shoals.

Snagboats

Sinkings caused by collisions with planters, sawyers, and floating logs were so common that the government established a fleet of boats specifically designed to remove the obstructions. These "snagboats" were double-hulled, double-engined sidewheelers. They

REMOVING A SNAG. A government snagboat lifts a tree trunk from the river. Huge trunks like this one littered the Lower Missouri and usually lodged in the river bottom as a planter or a sawyer. Snags could pierce the hull of an upward bound boat as easily as a knife pierces paper. Snags accounted for some 200 sinkings during the packet era.
(PHOTO COURTESY U.S. ARMY CORPS OF ENGINEERS.)

carried an iron hook and heavy tackle mounted to a derrick that towered between the hulls. A single snagboat would straddle the offending log, hook onto it, and yank it out, like a dentist extracting a tooth. Then the crewmen would saw up the log and let it drift harmlessly away or deposit it on shore. Snagging operations worked well, but there never were enough boats to go around. By the time a snagboat finished clearing its assigned district, a new invasion of impaled trees already had filled the river behind it. Records of the snagboat *Samson* indicated that she entered the Missouri in June, 1843. The river was so full of snags that it took her three months to get as far as Glasgow, 250 miles upriver. She was "outrooting" thirty snags a day on average, and by year's end had yanked out some 1,700 obstructions.

Stranding in low water

Low water was the bane of river navigation. The low stages came in midsummer and again during the winter. Western River steamboats were phenomenal for their shallow draft; even the largest first-class Missouri packets could clear the bottom in five feet of water. But at times the Missouri had no more depth than a farm pond. In very many places a man might wade all the way across the river without getting his hair wet, if the current were not there to sweep him away. Thus, when a boat ran aground—and all boats did run aground—the experienced crew knew immediately which method of several would work best to get her off.

The simplest method was towing. This required the presence of another boat—with an obliging captain. Boats routinely passed their stranded competition without stopping; there were no rules of chivalrous conduct on the river. When an offer was made to lend assistance it usually carried a steep cash price, payable in advance.

If the river showed signs of a rise, the captain of a stranded steamer might decide to save his money and let the coming swell sweep off his boat. It could take time; the captain would bear the expense of feeding the cabin passengers in the meantime, but a rise of mere inches often was enough to free the boat.

If a steamboat were not too hard aground, the crew could "kedge" it off. A kedge was a small anchor that could be transported in the boat's yawl. The yawl crew would pull ahead to a point beyond the shoal and drop the anchor; the other end of the kedge rope was then wrapped around the steamer's capstan. Using the combined power of the capstan and the engines, the boat literally pulled herself over the bar.

Another method consisted of lightening the boat by putting freight and sometimes passengers ashore in the yawl. In low water seasons many boats towed a "lighter" alongside. This lighter was either a barge or an old hull. The freight and fuel were divided between the steamboat and the lighter so that neither vessel drew too much water.

Sparring off

Still another method of extricating a vessel from shallow water was "sparring off." Sparring was an ingenious method commonly used on the Missouri. The spars were two thick poles, about thirty feet long, which normally were suspended by masts and booms on the left and right sides of the bow. The lower end of the spar was cut at a sharp angle; an eye-ring was attached to the upper end of each spar. A heavy pulley hung from the eye-ring, and it was connected by manila rope to a tackle block affixed on either side of the bow. The tail of the rope wound around the capstan. When the boat grounded, the crew lowered both spars into the

STEAMER *HELENA* AT MILK RIVER LANDING, MONTANA
TERRITORY, 1880. Two large sparring poles hang on either side of her bow,
and cords of fuel wood are stacked eight feet high on her main deck—telltale
signs of an upper river journey. The "P" device suspended between *Helena's*
smokestacks stands for the packet company that owned her—the Power Line of
Fort Benton. *Helena* hit a snag and sank near Chesterfield, Missouri, in 1891.

(PHOTO COURTESY MONTANA HISTORICAL SOCIETY.)

water until the sharp ends embedded themselves into the bottom. The spars were set so that they canted forward. Then, with the paddlewheels in motion, the crew tightened the ropes around the capstan, set it to turning, and the rope and pulleys lifted the boat upward and forward a few feet. The whole process was repeated, sometimes for days, until the boat had been "walked" over the bar. The position of the spars and booms reminded many observers of grasshopper legs, hence the practice frequently was called "grasshoppering."

Sparring off worked best when the boat was headed upstream. (The current usually swung the stern around on down bound vessels.) Sometimes the paddlewheels were turned in reverse during the process so as to dam up the river slightly. By turning against the current, the paddlewheels would force the water to back up and rise a few inches under the boat's hull, which could mean the difference between getting off and remaining stranded; the backward thrust of the wheels was minimal compared to the forward pull of the spars.

Samuel L. Clemens, who later would become famous as Mark Twain, rode up the Missouri River in 1861 as a passenger. He was an experienced Mississippi River pilot, but never had been on the Missouri. The river was low and up to its usual tricks. Regarding the frequent use of spars, Clemens wrote:

> We were six days going from St. Louis to "St. Joe" . . .. No record is left in my mind, now, concerning it, but a confused jumble of savage-looking snags, which we deliberately walked over with one [paddle] wheel or the other; and of reefs which we butted and butted, and then retired from and climbed over in some softer place; and of sandbars which we roosted on occasionally, and rested, and then got out our crutches and sparred over. In fact, the boat might almost as well have gone to St. Joe by land, for she was walking most of the time, anyhow—climbing over reefs and clambering over snags patiently and laboriously all day long.

A winter's journey

Though moody in all seasons, the river saved its meanest tricks for winter. The water was low. Like a spreading malignancy, snags and reefs hid just under the surface, awaiting their chance to kill the unwary steamboat. Ice drifted down from the north—not thin sheets, but boulders of ice, capable of crushing anything in its way. Ironically, winter was a season of heavy traffic in both passengers and freight. The combination of bad river and teeming business made for a miserable time afloat. Add to this the inherent danger of the Civil War in a border state, and one can easily understand why Charles Deatherage remembered a certain steamboat trip for the rest of his life:

> The writer was but a boy, and his father in St. Louis had seen Captain Charles Baker and made reservations for his family to be brought from Hill's Landing in Carroll County [Missouri] to St. Louis in November, 1864, and we arrived at the landing ready for our departure on Thursday.
>
> The *Sioux City* was probably having her troubles before reaching Kansas City, for she was more than four days behind her schedule in reaching our landing. On Sunday morning, while playing on the bank of the river, we saw issuing from the steam whistle that column of white steam so visible from an approaching boat, and thinking it the long-delayed *Sioux City*, we soon had our mother and the family assembled on the bank; it was but a few minutes until we discovered our mistake, as the trim little sternwheel steamer, the *Hattie May*, hove in sight, and tying up a few minutes, was soon gracefully gliding downstream; now drawing not more than three feet of water [she] had no difficulty in navigating over the bars.
>
> Tuesday morning we heard a well-known whistle as it gave us the landing warning—a long and two shorts. As the boat approached, swinging downstream, the famous name *Sioux City* was plainly visible in large black letters over the covering of the great sidewheels and soon she turned, headed upstream and gracefully glided into her berth at the landing. Two of the most agile roustabouts scrambled up the twenty-foot embankment with the great three-inch hawser to make her fast to the bank, and at the

same time some dozen or more were pushing the heavy stage plank to the top of that bank, and in a few moments we were on board and assigned to our comfortable staterooms, which had been reserved for us on a very crowded boat. A few hogsheads of tobacco were soon rolled down the gangplank, the bell sounded, and we were off for St. Louis.

Seeking the middle of the channel, as the Big Muddy, then very low, continued its tortuous course, now through some long chute near its bank where the great overhanging trees often swept near the deck, then again threading our way between the sandbars and the ever invisible snags, sometimes scraping the bottom. Our boat, loaded down to about four feet, had great difficulty in getting over many of the bars. The frequent taps of the bell calling for the heaving of the lead became very familiar to us, as the lead-heaver called out "f-i-v-e feet" and up to nine and a half feet, then "q-u-a-r-t-e-r l-e-s-s t-w-a-i-n" and "m-a-r-k t-w-a-i-n," when the bell was again tapped and the lead was called in. Often in touching the ledge of a bar he would sing out "t-h-r-e-e feet!" The lead-heavers were quite expert in their calling and were specialists in their line. We were told of an amusing incident on one of the boats, in which the regular lead-heaver was unavoidably off duty and a new man, of German proclivities, was ordered by the mate to handle the line. Not knowing any of the terms he cast out the line and sang out "much vater," and shortly afterwards, approaching shallow water, he called out "not much vater," and in a moment more the boat was on the bar, and when reprimanded by the mate he replied, "I told you there was not much vater."

[At Brunswick] the *Sioux City* was loaded down with many hogsheads of tobacco, and in the passenger list a woman and five children with scarlet fever were taken aboard. Resuming our journey on the *Sioux City* [we found ourselves] in a crowded boat and five children with scarlet fever, which spread to other children on the boat. The writer now has a sister who lost her hearing from that experience.

When the boat tied up at Glasgow, it was not long before Professor Strother escorted several young ladies of his academy down to see it, and among the number was an older sister of the writer. [Confederate Major General Sterling] Price had made his second raid through Missouri only one month before, and the battle of Glasgow was still fresh in the memory of the young ladies from Strother's Academy. [Price's subordinate, Brigadier] General Joe O. Shelby ordered Captain Collins' battery to open fire on the town from the Saline County side of the river, just at sunrise, and Shelby, taking Strother's Academy for the City Hall, in which he supposed the garrison was located, had directed Collins to fire at the

Academy. The first or second shot knocked off the northwest corner of the building. Professor Strother aroused his students, (and those girls probably dressed a little quicker than they had ever done before or have done since) and marshaling them in front of the building showed General Shelby his mistake, and he changed direction of the fire to the City Hall.

Our stay at Glasgow was prolonged on account of the very low stage of water, the captain preferring to take more time, as it was his last trip for the season, than risk his boat and cargo at night.

We were now well loaded as to tonnage, and also a very unwelcome passenger came aboard here, for he, too, was well loaded. This man was a soldier from a company of Missouri [Unionist] volunteers known as Merrill's Horse, and he gave us the greatest thrill of the entire trip. Unloosing from Glasgow at an early hour, we were soon approaching one of the most noted historic towns along the Missouri River, old Arrow Rock. But just before reaching it and while gliding smoothly down near the Saline County bank, this soldier, just sufficiently under the influence of liquor to stand upon his feet, yet knowing enough to make him feel brave, seeing several men on a high bluff from a quarter to a half mile away, he stepped over the guard rail on the cabin deck and emptied his revolver at them, and they, quickly accepting the challenge, returned the fire with their rifles.

The bells were rung for full steam ahead, and Captain Woolford lost no time at the wheel in changing that boat for the distant shore, while Captain Baker and his efficient clerk ordered the women and children to drop on the floor inside the cabin, and crouch down behind the walls of the staterooms. The minie balls flew thick for a few moments, some striking the pilothouse and smokestacks, but fortunately no one was hurt; but a week or more after, we read of the death of that member of Merrill's Horse, near Arrow Rock, where he left the boat.

The captain touched at Arrow Rock for only a few minutes, but about three miles below, the boat landed on a bar and we remained there three days and nights. It was here we had the experience of seeing the great spar poles used to their fullest extent, and realized they were not strung up on the bows of boats for ornament, and noted the power of the capstans when the great cables were wrapped round them, and as they were drawn taut how the great boat was moved around until it stood broadside across the stream. As the ice was running heavy, during the night it piled up against the boat, extending in a triangular shape for a hundred feet or more up the river, and packed tight, so that the stage planks were thrown out on it and plankways extended so the roustabouts could warm up as they attempted to cut us out. Their attempts were futile, and the *Sioux City* was thoroughly grounded and helpless, and might have been there yet if a rise of a foot in the river had not lifted us off the third night.

After this first rise in the river, the boat made fair progress for a day or two, until we reached the old Dutch* town of Hermann—when about three miles below we found the river spread out until there was no water that would carry us over. So we returned to Hermann and unloaded the heavy freight, such as hogsheads of tobacco, and the next day tried to cross the bar, without success. We again returned to Hermann and unloaded practically all the freight on the boat, and again tried the bar, only to find the only hope the captain had of landing his overcrowded boat of passengers was impossible. He again returned to Hermann and tied the boat up awaiting a rise in the river, and sent the passengers on the Missouri Pacific Railroad to St. Louis.

If you ever rode on a train in those days, when a water boy passed water through a tin pail, and heard the cries of those children with fevered brow, calling for water, as the scarlet fever patients suffered, you would realize how indelibly that trip on a Missouri River steamboat which failed to land us at our destination has been stamped so vividly on the writer's mind. We arrived in St. Louis about midnight, and the *Sioux City* came down about two weeks later.

Ice jams

In winter the Upper Missouri would freeze solid. On the lower river the frequent cycles of thawing and freezing would alternately open and close the river, but never so much as to render it absolutely safe from ice. Most steamboats left the Missouri in the winter, either to run on the Lower Mississippi, or put up at St. Louis for repairs and maintenance. But even at St. Louis ice could pose a problem. Sometimes it clogged the river and crowded upon itself like boulders at the base of a rock slide. A St. Louis newspaper reported on the condition of the Mississippi River on December 19, 1845, stating: "It is now fourteen days since the river closed, during which

---

* A corruption of the word *"Deutsche."* Hermann was a principal settlement of German immigrants in the two decades before the Civil War.

time persons have crossed freely on foot, and occasionally wagons and teams; but it has not been considered very safe to cross heavily loaded wagons." These ice jams—ice *dams,* really—could be several miles long and cause local upstream flooding. Eventually the weight of the rising river, coupled with moderating temperatures, would dislodge the dam. Then, without warning, the miniature icebergs would tumble down with the flood tide and smash anything that stood in the way. That exact situation took place on the Mississippi on February 27, 1856. Much of the pressure and surge that broke the ice came from the confluence of the Missouri River twenty miles above. Residents of St. Louis came to call the episode the "Break-up of '56." Their newspaper carried the story:

> The ice at first moved very slowly and without any perceptible shock. The boats lying above Chestnut Street were merely shoved ashore. Messrs. Eads' & Nelson's *Submarine Number 4,* which had just finished work at the wreck of the *Parthenia,* was almost immediately capsized and became herself a hopeless wreck. The *Submarine* floated down, lying broadside against the *Federal Arch,* which boat was being wrecked and of little value. Here the destruction commenced. The *Federal Arch* parted her fastenings and became at once a total wreck. Lying below were the steamers *Australia, Adriatic, Brunette, Paul Jones, Falls City, Altoona, A.B. Chambers,* and *Challenge,* all of which were torn away from the shore and in company with the *Submarine* and *Federal Arch,* floated down with the immense field of ice.
>
> The fleet of ten boats were more or less damaged at starting by crowding against one another. All the upper works of the *Brunette* and *Australia* were torn to pieces and the *Altoona* was badly damaged. The shock and the crushing of these boats when they were driven together can better be imagined than described. All their ample fastenings were as nothing against the enormous flood of ice, and they were carried down apparently fastened and wedged together. The first obstacles with which they came in contact were a large fleet of wood-boats, barges, and canal boats. These small fry were either broken to pieces or were forced out on the levee in a very damaged condition. We are not able to state the number, but there could not have been short of fifty in all, which were either sunk, broken, or carried away with the descending boats. About twenty of them met

with the latter fate, and the whole fleet lodged about one mile below, against the point of the island at the lower dike. The *Adriatic* lost one of her [paddle] wheels by swinging against the *Falls City* and the *Paul Jones*. The *Challenge* is also badly injured. After these boats passed down, the *Bon Accord* and *Highland Mary*, lying together, were carried off and are both a total loss. The new *St. Paul*, on the [dry] docks, was slightly damaged, and part of the docks swept away from under her. The *Highland Mary* struck against the *Die Vernon*, damaging the latter boat considerably. The *Louisville* was also torn away from her moorings, and at last accounts was lying broadside and across the current with the other boats below. She is probably a total loss. The *Lamartine* was carried away in the same manner and will doubtless be lost. The *Westerner* broke her fastenings and swung against the *Jeanie Deans*, injuring the latter considerably.

Some of the boats lying above Chestnut Street fared badly in the meantime. The *F.X. Aubrey* was forced into the bank and had her larboard wheel broken. The noble *Nebraska*, which everyone thought in a most perilous position, lost her larboard wheel and was not otherwise injured. The *Gossamer, Luella, Alice,* and *Badger State* were forced ashore and slightly damaged. Both the Alton wharf boats were sunk and broken to pieces. The old *Shenandoah*, being wrecked, and the *Sam Cloon* were forced away from shore and floated down together against the steamer *Clara*. The latter did not part her fastenings, and she and the *Shenandoah* lodged, when they were soon torn to pieces and sunk by the ice and one of the ferryboats, which came down alone. The ferryboat floated on to the foot of Market Street, carrying part of the *Shenandoah* with her. The steamers *Clara* and *Ben Bolt* were both badly damaged by the ice and forced partly ashore. The *G.W. Sparhawk* was sunk, and looked as if broken in two lying at the shore. The Keokuk wharf boat maintained its position against the flood and saved three boats below, the *Polar Star, J.S. Pringle,* and *Forest Rose,* none of which were up to this time materially injured.

After running about one hour, the character of the ice changed, and it came down in a frothy, crumbled condition, with now and then a heavy piece. At the end of two hours it ran very slowly, and finally stopped about half-past five o'clock. During this interval a number of persons crossed it from the ferry landing on Bloody Island. They were chiefly passengers by a train just arrived, anxious to reach the city. The experiment was daring, but they landed safely on this side.

Just before the river gorged, huge piles of ice twenty and thirty feet in height were forced up by the current on every hand, both on the shore and at the lower dike, where so many boats had come to a halt. In fact these boats seemed to be literally buried in ice. It had not been broken below Cahokia Bend, and all the drift thus far had gorged between the city and that point; hence its sudden stop. At six o'clock p.m. the river had risen at least ten feet. At dark the people went home.

The terrible sweep of waters with its burden of ice, the mashing to pieces of boats, the hurrying to and fro of the excited crowd, was one of the most awful and at the same time most imposing scenes we have ever witnessed. The officers and crews of many of the boats went down the river with them; the lookers-on became alarmed and sprang from boat to boat in a rush for the shores. The captains and owners of canal, flatboats, and barges fled, leaving their property to the mercy of circumstances. At seven p.m. the gorge below broke and the ice began running again. The current was now much more swift and the night very dark, a heavy and steady rain having set in.

Missouri River tributaries

Many large tributaries fed the Missouri, but few were navigable by steamboat. The Missouri itself was formed by the junction of three smaller streams in Montana: the Jefferson, Madison, and Gallatin Rivers. In descending order, the major tributaries of the Missouri were the Milk, Yellowstone, Cheyenne, James, Platte, Kansas (commonly called the Kaw), Grand, Chariton, Osage, and Gasconade. A few steamboats ran on the Yellowstone—and even its tributary, the Big Horn—as support vessels for military campaigns against Indians, but these runs were infrequent and limited to a very short season. The Platte was the longest tributary of the Missouri. Parallel to its banks ran the Oregon Trail and, later, the transcontinental railroad; but the meandering, island-flecked Platte normally was too shallow to admit steamboats.

Steamboats on the Gasconade and Osage Rivers

Only the Gasconade and Osage Rivers, down in Missouri, hosted steam navigation on a regular basis. The Gasconade was navigable for some 70 miles to near Vienna. Due to its scenic beauty, the Gasconade was popular for excursion trips which originated at Hermann on the Missouri River. There was just enough freight to keep a few boats operating on the Gasconade in season, and at least one boat obtained a contract to carry the mail.

The nearby Osage was open most of the year from its mouth, just below Jefferson City, to Linn Creek, a distance of 113 river miles, and to Warsaw, 172 miles, during the seasonable wet weather of spring and early summer. Over the centuries, the winding Osage had cut deeply into its bed of limestone and dolomite, leaving a narrow valley flanked by high hills and sheer cliffs. From the days of earliest human habitation the Osage had a reputation for dramatic rises, but never more so than during the record flood of 1844.

There was a legend involving St. Clair County, Missouri, and the great flood of 1844. The hill people of St. Clair County lived isolated lives—roads were few and difficult. The Osage River meandered through the county but steamboats never ventured that high up. One day a frightened farmer came riding into the tiny settlement of Papinsville and spread the story that some mysterious animal had scared him away from his work. He had not seen the beast, he said, and did not care to, judging from the sound of its awful, howling scream. Folks listened in hushed amazement to his story, but didn't know what to make of it, for nobody else had heard a thing. Next morning, though, not long after sunrise, the wild screams began anew—and this time the whole town heard it. The menfolk fetched their guns and dogs and set off after the thing. It was coming from away off down the valley, moving one way and then the other, distant at times, then nearer. Every time the monster let off a scream the dogs would perk up and howl and run about trying to pick up a scent; yet they never could. Along toward sundown the creature grew quiet. The hunters took shelter

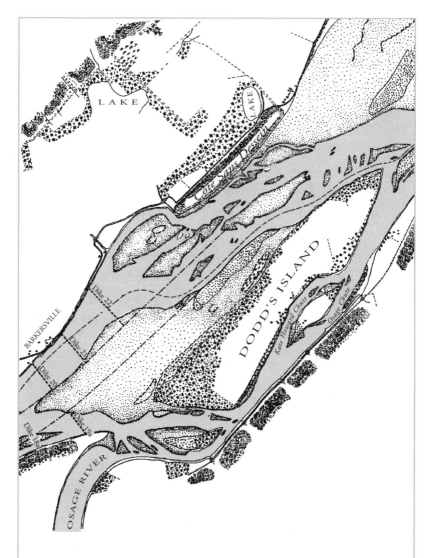

Confluence
of the Missouri and Osage Rivers, 1891

An obstacle course of islands and sandbars—a pilot's nightmare.
Note Kate Howard Chute, named after a boat that sank there in
1859.
(FROM THE MISSOURI RIVER COMMISSION, MAP OF MISSOURI RIVER, 1891.)

in a cave near a sharp bend of the river. Next morning, sure enough, the fearful scream began again, and moved steadily nearer until it seemed as though the thing must be just around the point. The hunters placed themselves behind some timber with their guns cocked and ready. A few amongst them, fearing the worst, put their rifles aside and stood with drawn knives. Breathlessly they waited; the thing drew so close they could hear it snorting. Suddenly it swung into plain view in the center of the river: the *Flora Jones,* first steamboat ever to climb the Osage River into St. Clair County!

In 1906—still within the steamboat era—the government constructed a lock and dam on the Osage, 12 miles above its mouth. This 9-foot high structure formed a pool sufficient for the operation of steam towboats on the lower river throughout the warm weather months. The construction of Bagnell Dam, beginning in 1929, and the subsequent formation of Lake of the Ozarks, confined commercial navigation thereafter to the lower 82 miles of the Osage.

Tie rafting on the Osage

For a time, the Osage carried a considerable amount of non-powered traffic. From the 1870s to the 1920s, the adjoining Osage River Hills fostered a lively timber industry. The timber was cut for railroad ties that were then assembled into large rafts and floated down the river to the railhead at Bagnell or Osage City.

Floating on a raft of railroad ties had its pleasant moments, especially when the river was falling. Raftsmen learned that a falling river was slightly lower in the middle than along the sides, hence the rafts tended to stay in the channel without much trouble. But when the Osage got too low, there was no channel. The steamboats couldn't run and even tie rafts had a hard time getting through. The following excerpt, written by Jefferson D. Blount, illustrates the difficulty of getting tie rafts over the shoals:

> I was 18 years old and it was at the toe of Horseshoe Bend, just below Cape Galena. We put in ten thousand ties, started down the river on the 15th day of August, 1879, and we was 31 days on the trip [to Osage City].
>
> The river was at a dead low stage, and the first day we got to Mining Port Shoal, a distance of three miles. There we had to cut free the first raft and make dams out of it so we could get through with the other rafts. Then we had to pry the first over with hand spikes. My, but it was hard work. We had to lift all we could and then some more, and I mean we had one hell of a time at Mining Port.
>
> When we got to Brockman Ford we had to go out to the farmers and borrow brush hooks to cut the moss out of the shoal before we could get through. We were three days on the shoal, that made us five days on the road, a distance of 16 miles. After we were on the river about ten days, our feet were all water poisoned, swelled as round as a pole and the blood would ooze through the skin. If they had been scalded they could not have hurt worse. I said if I ever got home alive, I would stay on the farm.
>
> Thirty days after we had started, we sighted Osage City, 4 miles distance. I never was so proud to see a place as I was to see that place . . . . But oh my, it was hell on the Osage.

Steamboats on the Little Platte and Grand Rivers

Steamboat captains, being men accustomed to taking chances, occasionally attempted to get their boats up other tributaries of the Missouri. The Grand, Chariton, and Kaw saw a few boats in seasons of high water. The steamers that tried these rivers necessarily would have been very small. There were tremendous risks in running narrow and shoal streams; if the boat became stranded it might rot there before the next heavy rain came along. But there was always the promise of a hefty freight consignment on the down bound trip from the farmers and merchants of small and otherwise isolated villages. And sometimes there were additional incentives. In the wet spring of 1843 the steamer Colonel Woods made it a few miles up the Little Platte River to Platte City, Missouri. Together with freight revenue, the captain of the boat received a $300 prize which the citizens of Platte City had set aside for just such an occasion. Platte City was not alone in its quest for commercial success via the river. In the 1844 flood another steamer made a run to Chillicothe, Missouri, located 40 miles up the Grand River. The water was at record high stages, and not likely to rise to those levels again for years, but the denizens of Chillicothe were certain that this marked the beginning of great things for their town. Newspapers as far away as St. Louis exhorted local politicians to petition the government for money to clear a permanent channel on the Grand. The state legislature responded with a meaningless resolution that declared Grand River navigable all the way to the Iowa line. But the money—well, the money never came. The railroads eventually did, and the channel improvement idea was forgotten. Those brief moments of heady speculation which seized Platte City, Chillicothe, and numerous other tributary towns provided a theme for the Mark Twain novel, The Guilded Age.

3

Working
on the River

ST. LOUIS LEVEE, CIRCA 1846. One of the earliest known photographs of the St. Louis waterfront shows some 28 steamers wedged in along the macadamized levee—a common scene throughout the period of 1840 to 1860. Note the absence of a texas on most of the boats. The texas was a new adaptation at the time and seen only on the newest and best-appointed steamers. (PHOTO COURTESY U.S. ARMY CORPS OF ENGINEERS.)

Crew complement

As many as 80 persons, male and female, could be employed on a single packet boat—a very large packet boat. A more typical Missouri River steamer might carry a crew of forty or less; the number would vary according to the size of the vessel, the level of passenger service deemed necessary by the owners, and the amount of freight handled. At times the crew outnumbered the passengers.

On a Missouri River packet of the mid-nineteenth century, the officers consisted of a captain, two pilots, a chief clerk, a steward, two engineers, and two mates. The clerk, pilots, and engineers were permitted the luxury—or burden, depending on their point of view—of employing apprentices. On large boats these young apprentices were considered officers-in-training, much like naval midshipmen.

The clerk's apprentices—there could be two or more—were titled second clerks, or, more often, "mud clerks." The latter name derived from the fact that they went ashore with consignment papers or bills of lading at every freight stop—whether paved city wharf or muddy plantation landing. Pilots had their steersmen, or "cubs," a calling made famous in Mark Twain's *Life on the Mississippi*. The engineers' apprentices were the "strikers." Theirs was a hard, thankless job made more difficult by the constant maintenance tasks required of the boiler and engine components.

In addition to managing their apprentices, some boats' officers also superintended the regular crew. Engineers supervised the firemen. The normal complement was one stoker per boiler per watch. Mates directed the work of the deckhands and roustabouts. Deckhands were the able seamen of the rivers. They manned the yawls, set spars, ran out the lines, secured barges and lighters, and assisted in the general maintenance and operation of the vessel. Passengers often confused them with roustabouts, or "rousters." (On some smaller boats the distinction was blurred.) Rousters were the manual laborers who loaded the freight and wood. A large steamboat might carry thirty or more rousters per trip.

The steward, a well-paid officer of the boat, oversaw the work of the cooks and waiters, and assumed responsibility for the porters, cabin boys, and chambermaids.

Other positions on a boat included a carpenter, to repair the frequent damage done by logs and rough handling; a barkeeper, who worked under contract and supplied his own stores and assistant; and a watchman, whose duties ranged from security guard to errand boy. In post-emancipation days, with all crew members drawing a salary, a captain could expect to pay some $3,000 per month in wages.

Pilots and piloting

The riverboat pilot was an American classic. He ranked with cowboys and railroad engineers as an enduring symbol of the romance of the Western frontier. But the pilot had the better of it, for he was at least as independent as the cowboy and far better paid than the engineer. The pilot was a professional contractor, not an

THE BRAIDED CHANNEL OF THE UPPER MISSOURI. The nineteenth
century river never remained the same for long. In the interval of a single day,
whole islands and bars might change shape or disappear completely. A popular
adage of the time held that the great uncertainties of life were the state of a
woman's mind and the condition of the Missouri River.

(PHOTO COURTESY U.S. ARMY CORPS OF ENGINEERS.)

employee of a boat or packet line. In busy times he could stipulate
his own terms. Pilots signed on for a trip or for a season and captains frequently paid extra to retain a competent pilot through the
off season. Pilots enjoyed the greatest prosperity in the decade
before the Civil War; their wages reached $300 per month—an
exquisite salary matched by no other profession. The successful
pilot had to possess an extraordinary memory, steady nerves, and
the ability to read the river and anticipate its tricks. Pilots also
loved to talk about themselves and their trade; it took only a ques-
tion or two to warm them to their task. Upon assurance that we
have broken no protocol, we humbly enter the pilothouse with a
magazine writer of 1870, and stand in awe to observe the icon of
Americana in his element:

> Of all that belongs to life on our great Western Rivers, the business
> and experiences of the pilots interest me most; and, as they are to have

our lives in keeping for twelve hundred miles to come, it is worth our while to know all about them. No class of public servants stand in a position of greater trust and responsibility than theirs. The captain of our boat, for example, has supreme command, and is held responsible for the doings of all those within his control, but his authority is, in fact, limited in the pilothouse; for, although he has the power of directing the action of the pilot, yet, so far as taking this or that direction is concerned, he seldom exercises it. I cannot conceive of a more arduous and dangerous business than that of guiding one of these majestic steamboats along the twisting, shifting, treacherous channel of the river. The ocean steamship, whatever may happen, has the refuge of the open sea. The direction to be pursued is well known, and the compass points the way, while, if the vessel is deprived of the use of steam, she can resort to canvas, and, beyond delay, but little injury occurs. The man who directs the movement of the locomotive may, by the slightest carelessness, cause the death of hundreds of his fellow beings; yet most accidents by railroad happen from exterior and accidental causes. There are many other stations in life where the safety of human beings and of property is dependent upon the judgment and good conduct of a single man. But in neither one nor all of them is there any such grave responsibility as that resting upon the pilot of the Western River. Truly must he be a man of rare natural gifts of memory of localities, quick observing comprehension, a sure hand, rapid judgment, determination of will, iron nerve, even temper, and good habits.

Let the reader imagine himself perched sixty feet above the water in the pilothouse, which is a good-sized box, usually ten or fifteen feet square, built up high above the cabins of the boat, and somewhere near its center. This lofty aerie is enclosed upon all sides with glass windows, so that the pilot at the wheel, which is a big thing, may see both shores and up and down the river. Our pilot is surrounded by speaking tubes, and bell ropes. There are two engines, so that there are duplicate bell ropes. They signal "stop her"; "go ahead"; "back her"; "slow"; "fast," and what not, so that although fifty feet or more of space and half a dozen decks separate the pilot from the engineer, yet they are as one man, or one is the double of the other.

Piloting proved to be more art than science. It was taught by word of mouth and reinforced with hands-on training. A pilot would tell his cub that the only book to read was the river itself. "Reading" the river meant the ability to discern the water's depth by careful observation of the motion and appearance of the river's surface. The clues were subtle and easily misread by an inexperienced pilot. For example, it was an accepted fact that higher waves formed over the deepest water. This was a simple way to judge relative depth. A careless or new pilot might steer for those higher waves without giving the situation a second thought. But this rule of thumb only applied when the wind was coming from upstream; if the wind came from the opposite direction then high waves meant shallow water.

Reefs were always a concern for the pilot. A reef was an underwater ledge. It formed when silt-laden water deflected off a stationary object such as an island, a point, a cluster of snags, or even an old wreck. Usually a reef presented a shallow incline on its upstream side and would rise to within a few feet of the surface. On its downstream side it formed an almost perpendicular wall which dropped ten feet or more. A down bound boat might pass over a reef with no trouble save for a little grinding on the hull. If an up bound boat, however, hit the bluff side of the same reef the force of the impact would crush its hull. Most reefs extended outward only a short distance from a prominent point on the bank. In that case a boat could run around the end of a reef. But not so with a rainbow reef; it derived its name from the long arc that it formed as it extended all the way across the river. There was always a "break" in the reef—something akin to a miniature mountain pass—through which a boat could pass without striking the reef. The difficulty was in finding the break; sometimes it could be located only by sounding the river bottom with a weighted line.

Then there were crossings. Between any two bends the channel crossed over and the steamboat had to follow. Some crossings were deeper than others, some were more easily read than others, but there were few crossings that a pilot took for granted. While taking his boat from one side to the other the pilot had to be especially alert for slick, flat-looking places on the water: this meant a bar was forming just under the surface. A rolling, boiling area also could spell trouble, for this lesion marked the remains of a bar that was washing away in the shifting current. The Missouri River so frequently changed its course that the pilot could not rely on memory alone—he had to see the water, clearly. For this reason steamboats seldom ran the river at night except in a very bright phase of the moon. It was considered unwise to run during a rainstorm, for the rippling pattern of the raindrops camouflaged all the signs on the surface. Nor would a boat run in the fog.

Good piloting also required that the pilot know how to handle his boat. A pilot had to anticipate the "swing" of his vessel and stay ahead of her, or else she would "run away" from him. Sometimes the simple act of heading a boat downstream could cure a body of ever wishing to be a pilot. It always was harder to steer a down bound boat: the vessel needed more speed to maintain steerageway. Pilots grew old prematurely by taking a boat at twelve or fifteen miles per hour down a channel they scarcely could perceive. In order to avoid this, some pilots turned the boat around and backed through especially difficult reaches and bends. One pilot had the signature habit of allowing his down bound boat to gently run aground at the head of a sandbar so the current would swing it around and he could back it down past the bar.

Many tales of old-time piloting came from the lucid pen and peaked curiosity of professional writers who rode the boats and found themselves enthralled by the easy conversation of the pilothouse. Typically, the writers were oblivious to the channel and were amazed to see the pilot swing his boat back and forth across a wide river rather than steer straight down the middle. Upon inquiry the pilot patiently would explain that he was following the line of deeper water—following it by signs that were as obvious to him as they were obscure and mysterious to the writer. One perplexed correspondent, after examining the water very carefully and trying to guess which way the boat would turn, finally gave up and asked the pilot how he did it. The pilot replied: "Well, it's sort of instinct. I can tell something of the color of the water, something by its motion, and something in the habits of the beast; and between 'em all I manage to find my way."

By virtue of the responsibility and trust bestowed upon pilots, their craft was one of the first professions to be regulated by the United States government. After passage of the landmark Steamboat Inspection Act of 1852, the fine print on every pilot's license reminded the holder of his duties, and the penalties for ignoring them. For example, any steersman working alone who was not fully licensed to operate a passenger steamboat was subject to a (then) stiff fine of one hundred dollars for each occurrence. Any pilot who was deemed incompetent, or who placed his boat and passengers in peril through misconduct or neglect, could lose his license permanently; and anyone who was injured through the misconduct or neglect of a pilot could sue that pilot for damages. It was the duty of all pilots to point out any defects in the hull or steam apparatus of their vessels to government inspectors. Failure to do so could result in the revocation of the pilot's license. (Conversely, compliance with this rule just as easily could result in the pilot's dismissal by the boat's owner.) Pilots also were required to report all serious accidents to the inspectors, regardless of culpability. Finally, as defined by the wording on their licenses, pilots were divided into three categories. First-class pilots were qualified to act as chief pilot on any boat by virtue of "long experience in the navigation and management of all classes of steam vessels." Second-class pilots, whose experiences were more limited, could work as chief pilot on medium or small vessels, but only could serve as relief, or second, pilot on the largest steamboats. (Large steamers were defined as vessels that registered over 750 tons displacement.) The lowest category was that of assistant pilot—the cubs. They were "not considered to have sufficient knowledge of the route," and never were to be left "in charge of the deck."

The white-knuckle aspect of the pilots' profession may have provided some explanation for the personal flamboyance and excesses that seemed prevalent in the brotherhood. Certainly, many of them were solid family men of temperate and unassuming ways. But there were plenty of high rollers in the craft and the stories told about them outlived the flush times in which they worked. When Grant Marsh, former pilot and master, dictated his memoirs in 1909, he made a point to include a few tales about the truly legendary pilots of his day:

> One of these was Joe Oldham, a man famous in his time for three things: his skill as a pilot, his independence, and his extravagance in personal adornment. His was the distinction of possessing the largest, heaviest, and most expensive gold watch on the river. Its stem contained a diamond worth five hundred dollars, and he wore huge fur mittens reaching to his elbows, and in the summer kid gloves of the most delicate hue.
>
> One day a small, sidewheel packet, the *Moses Greenwood,* on her way up from the Ohio bound for Weston, Missouri, came into St. Louis looking for a Missouri River pilot. It happened that Oldham was the only one in town and when the captain came to him, he blandly stated that he would take the *Moses Greenwood* to Weston and back, about a week's trip, for one thousand dollars. The captain demurred, but after several days, during which no other pilots appeared, and being in a hurry, he went to Oldham and said that the would pay the price.
>
> "Well, I can't accept now, Captain," answered the pilot nonchalantly. "I'm going to a picnic this afternoon."
>
> Pleadings were of no avail, and to the picnic he went.
>
> On another occasion the steamer *Post Boy,* Captain Rider, came into St. Louis on her way to Leavenworth. Captain Rider sent for Oldham, who was again the only member of the craft in town, and he came down

to the levee, bedecked with diamonds as usual, wearing a silk hat and patent leather shoes, and shielding himself from the summer sun with a gold-handled, silk umbrella.

"How much will you charge to take my boat to Leavenworth and back, Mr. Oldham?" asked the captain.

"Fifteen hundred dollars," answered the pilot, gently.

"What?" shouted Captain Rider. "Man, that's more than the boat will make."

Oldham shrugged his shoulders.

"Well, talk fast, Captain," he said. "I won't stand here in the hot sun fifteen minutes for fifteen hundred dollars."

The captain ground his teeth, but there was nothing to be done save pay the price or lie in port. So at length he said: "All right, I'll consent to be robbed this time. We're all ready to start. Come aboard."

"But I'm not ready," quoth the pilot. "Just call a carriage and send me up to my rooms for my baggage."

Nevertheless, once aboard he did his work well, making the round trip in the excellent time of nine days and with no mishaps from the pitfalls of the treacherous Big Muddy. Despite all the money he earned during the years of the river's prosperity, when it was over, poor, improvident Oldham found himself penniless, and when he died, years after, it was in abject poverty, in a wretched hovel near the river bank at Yankton, South Dakota.

It was fortunate for Captain Rider in his transaction with Oldham, that the latter was not of as sensitive a disposition as the pilot in another similar case. This man's name was Bob Burton and one day when the steamer *Aleonia,* Captain Miller, appeared at St. Louis, Bob demanded one thousand dollars for taking her to Weston, with the result that Captain Miller called him a robber and ordered him off the boat. As usual, the captain could secure no one else, and after several days, sent for Bob and told him that he would pay the thousand dollars.

"I won't go for less than fifteen hundred," replied Bob.

"What?" growled the captain. "You said you'd go for a thousand."

"Yes," said Bob, "but you insulted me, sir, and I charge you five hundred dollars for that."

Whatever the wages they could command, the pilots were not always entirely successful in navigating the difficult Missouri, but they seldom permitted themselves to be criticized or to appear disconcerted even in the face of repeated mishaps for which they were responsible. This was aptly demonstrated in the case of a certain member of the craft who once, in steering a boat up from St. Louis, met with so many accidents such as running aground, breaking the wheel, and otherwise mutilating the vessel, that at last the captain came to him angrily and demanded: "Look here, how many times have you been up the Missouri River, anyway?"

"Twice," responded the navigator unabashed. "Once in a skiff and once on horseback."

Another [pilot] of the early days was Jim Gunsalis, who almost rivaled Oldham in the barbaric splendor of his apparel. When he was pilot of the *A.B. Chambers No. 2,* his regular salary was eight hundred dollars per month. His particular weakness was for diamonds. Though the cabin was always so filled with passengers that the officers of the boat were accustomed to take their meals in the texas, Gunsalis positively refused to do so, insisting on a seat at the saloon table, where his jewelry might receive its due meed of admiration. He, like Oldham, died in poverty, his last occupation being that of a tender pilot for a dump boat at Carondelet, below St. Louis, and his funeral expenses were paid by subscription.

Perhaps because all pilots were perceived as rich and eccentric—and a bit unapproachable—the public enjoyed a good laugh at their expense. So it was when the popular *Harper's New Monthly Magazine* circulated a tale about an unnamed pilot in 1870. Whether it was fact or fiction was not important; it was funny because it proved that pilots were just as human as everyone else:

> It was in the summer, and on a trip up the river. A corpse had been taken on board . . . , and for safety's sake, and because it was cooler there, it was placed in the pilothouse. The pilot was not altogether temperate. In fact, a cocktail was necessary to his happiness at least every half hour, and he made an arrangement with the barkeeper by which, after midnight, he had possession of the key to the bar, so that he could go or send down for his own cocktail. As midnight approached he began to get rather nervous about his corpse, and all the ghost stories he had ever heard came thronging before him with intense reality. Now and then he would look over his shoulder at the coffin, which stood upright against the window, and the sight did not reassure him.
>
> Suddenly, for an instant, he turned his eyes from the river, and at his very elbow he saw a figure in white which held up a bony finger, as if in warning, while ghostly, hollow eyes stared into his. That one look was enough; for, fully possessed with the belief that the ghost of the man dead

in the coffin stood beside him, he gave one frantic scream, and, at a single jump, sprang over the wheel and through the window on to the roof of the cabin, twenty feet below.

It subsequently required the presence of the ghost in person to persuade our poor pilot that he was only the barkeeper, who had forgotten to send up the key of the bar until after he had gone to bed, and so came up, silently, in his bare feet, shirt, and drawers.

Cubbing

Cubbing on the Missouri was a slow and informal undertaking when compared to the more precise and sustained education of a Mississippi pilot. The Missouri was much harder to learn and at least as difficult to navigate. A pilot might run a given stretch of the Upper Missouri only twice per year, compared to twice a month or more on the Mississippi. But many Mississippi pilots longed for the chance to get a Missouri River endorsement on their license despite the inconvenience and expense involved. By one account a Missouri River pilot on a run from Saint Louis to Fort Benton could make fifteen hundred dollars a month and as much as ten thousand dollars a season for a single trip. These were extremely high wages even in a profession where good pay was the rule. In order to gain experience on the Upper Missouri a young pilot or cub would have to find a first-class pilot willing to take him on, and for this the student would pay his mentor up to five hundred dollars for one trip. The cub also would have to pay for his own expenses during the trip, as the boat's captain was not inclined to feed the cub free of charge.

Late in his life, William L. Heckmann, Jr., published his memoirs of cubbing and piloting on the Missouri. Heckmann was born into a riverboat family: his father and uncle were pilots and boat owners. The younger Heckmann started working as a cub in 1882.

By that time the era of packet boats had ended and most of his experience came on steam towboats, freight boats, and small excursion boats.

Heckmann told of standing in the pilothouse day after day watching the pilot steer the boat. After several months of this he finally was allowed to take the wheel himself, but only in a safe, deep stretch of river. From this point on he was expected to master a series of progressively more difficult situations: he had to learn how to shave the boat close to the shore on upstream trips in order to take advantage of slack current; he was expected to take the boat through a series of crossings, each more challenging than the last; he had to acquaint himself with the intricacies of landing the boat—first a simple upstream landing, which was not so simple if a backeddy took hold of the boat, then a downstream landing which required the pilot to swing the boat around in mid-stream before nosing her into the shore. All of this would have been harrowing enough in the best of circumstances, but pilots of the old days would test the coolness of their cubs by shouting and cursing at them in the midst of their efforts. Many a cub, be it Bill Heckmann or Sam Clemens, must have questioned their resolve in choosing such a demanding and unforgiving profession for their life's work.

Henry Blossom, mud clerk

Many a successful businessman got his start as a mud clerk on a river steamer. The variety of work, fair pay, and ample travel appealed to young lads who hoped to obtain a foothold in the realm of free enterprise. Indeed, clerks often became shareholders in their boats and would someday own a vessel outright, either as captain or shore-bound entrepreneur. First, though, they had to endure an initial trial as an apprentice clerk—a time when all was new and the world lay before them; but it could be a frustrating and exceedingly lonesome time, as well. For a look at the life of a young steamboat clerk, and the routine business of steamboating, we now peruse the journal of one Henry Martyn Blossom—twenty years old, reared in Madison, New York, and about to finish a year as second clerk on the Missouri River steamer *Polar Star.* For reasons that soon will become obvious, we will entitle his musings: "The Diary of a Lovelorn Youth"—

> [In port, St. Louis,] Sunday, August 4th, 1853. In the morning I wrote to Sarah Stillman and then attended Reverend Elliot's church. Went home to dinner. In the afternoon I was most agreeably surprised with the appearance of Mr. Riddlebarger. He invited me to call on his lady—formerly Miss Sarah J. Finch—an invitation which I gladly accepted. Although my acquaintance with her had been exceedingly limited—amounting barely to an introduction—I enjoyed one of the pleasantest of short visits. It seemed good to be in the presence of a Yankee girl once more. At 7:30 o'clock we adjourned to Church of Messiah. Then I went down to the *Polar Star* feeling very queer and perplexed with all sorts of odd thoughts. *The Star* wasn't shining then.
>
> Monday, September 5th. In the morning I commenced a letter . . . which I did not finish, as interruptions were too frequent and the freight began to come down thicker and faster.
>
> Tuesday. Rain came up about noon and stopped me for awhile from receiving freight, and did not leave until 6 o'clock in the evening, or thereabouts. Raining very hard when we shoved off.
>
> Wednesday had nothing in it of interest. We got a big log in the wheel just above Jefferson City and had to stop and cut it out—and during the night cut snags for the boat to pass. In the morning found ourselves considerably behind our times.
>
> Thursday. Put off Mr. and Mrs. Riddlebarger at Glasgow. I only saw her once during the trip. She was in bed most of the time. Something very singular characterized the conduct of both.
>
> Saturday. [Reached] St. Joseph 7 p.m.
>
> In port, Friday, September 16, 1853. The down trip [from St. Joseph to St. Louis], which terminated last evening at 8 o'clock, was a very pleasant one indeed. We brought 150 passengers to this city, large portion of

whom were ladies, besides our usual compliment of way passengers who landed at points above. Among the more agreeable circumstances, I might mention the presence of Miss Lizy Summers, who has made several trips on the *Polar Star*, and was then on her way home to Flemingsburg, Fleming County, Kentucky. Miss Sarah Leach . . . was on board. I was by no means as favorably impressed with the appearance of the said lady as the very enthusiastic encomiums of Mr. W. had led me to expect. She is what in very expressive though vulgar parlance might be termed "green!" But it is a happy thing that all do not see alike. Last evening Miss Leach and Mr. Summers, Miss Summers, and myself went up to Rimmer's where the time passed very pleasantly over two glasses of ice cream, after which we took a decidedly agreeable promenade by the full and very glorious light of the moon.

Saturday, September 17, 1853. The day has been as monotonous as such a day in port usually is, with the exception that I received in the afternoon a "right smart" lot of freight. Last night and this evening I went up to sister Laura's and ate bountifully of that notoriously excellent Hoosier dish—fried chicken—and the timely accompaniment of delicious peaches.

Sunday, 18th. This morning I took a thorough ablution and then attended the Church of Messiah services, as usual. After eating of Laura's fried chicken and peach pies, I returned to the boat and wrote another long letter. In the evening, a hard rain "estopped" me from going to church, and I sat on the after guards, watching the copious falling sheet until the mosquitoes became an intolerable nuisance and obliged me to retire. I sought bed early with a feeling of loneliness to which I do not often give way.

Monday, September 19th, 1853. During the day I received small lots of freight as they came down, and did not place my signature to the last dray ticket until quite dark. I then went up to the Varieties [Theater] to see the attractions of the day. For two or three nights past I have slept in the pilothouse—the cool, fresh breeze furnishing a better indemnity against mosquitoes, the "petty plagues" of the season, than the mosquito bars down in the closer air of my stateroom. The moon, now in its decline, shone there full in my face, bringing back to me old memories, intense thought, and a most disturbing feeling of loneliness. One of the city's inimitable German bands was practicing, just across the levee, "Sounds from Home" and other home airs. The exquisite sweetness of the music, falling upon the still air and reverberating in most melodious accent all along the river, did not serve to banish thought.

The Cutoff at Brunswick Bend

BEFORE 1875 —————————————————————————

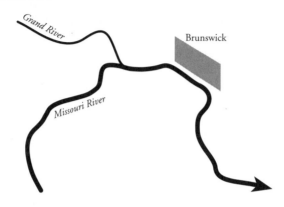

AFTER 1875 —————————————————————————

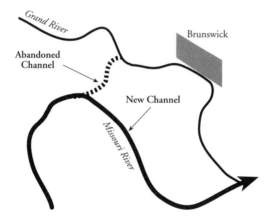

The Missouri River once flowed directly in front of Brunswick, Missouri. Due to high water in 1875, the river abandoned its old channel and cut a new bed more than 2 miles southeast of Brunswick. The Grand River, which had flowed into the Missouri just above Brunswick, now filled the old channel in front of the town. Hence, without moving, the once busy river port of Brunswick found itself entirely off the Missouri and *4 miles up the Grand River!*

Tuesday, 20th. We left port at 5:30 p.m. with about 80 or 90 passengers on board, and having a fair freight which put us down to four feet.

Up trip, Wednesday, September 21st. We made a very good run last night but lost time during the day. We grounded only once—at Bennett's—at the foot of which the *Robert Campbell* was "banking" her freight. While we were rubbing on the bottom—which seems to have gotten very near the top—the *Campbell* came up and got stuck. The *Banner State*, coming down, also stuck; so that there were three boats aground within a few feet of each other at the same time. We soon got off—setting our spar only twice—and discharged freight.

Thursday, September 22d, 1853. We had a thick fog for 10 hours last night and this morning, and are consequently a good deal behind our time. We were in Boonville about dinner time, at Glasgow in the afternoon, and at Brunswick about 10 o'clock in the evening.* I expected to see Mr. Riddlebarger at Glasgow, but he was not observable, and as I subsequently learned, went up on the *St. Ange*. His wife don't like Kansas [City].

Saturday, September 24th. We were at Weston about 10 o'clock this morning and reached St. Joseph soon after "early candle-lighting," as I used to hear the parsons say.

Sunday, 25th. I discharged my freight, went up to the *Gazette* office, and came back to the boat. I did not feel very well. As soon as the "spirit moved me," I commenced a letter to Sue Brigham, which I succeeded in elongating considerably.

Monday, September 26th. We left St. Joe with a very fair trip of passengers, which received considerable accessions at Weston in the afternoon. My old acquaintance Miss McDonald—who would not cry over Eva's imaginary death in *Uncle Tom*—I had expected to go down with us as far as Lexington, but I believe she was too late for the boat. She "waited for the wagon too long," and so missed the adventure so full of promise.

Tuesday, September 27th. We are full of passengers—among whom was General Milburn's daughter, a St. Louis "garl," and very evidently a confirmed coquette. We laid up for the night at Richfield, our detentions by the way having stopped us at that point. We had a brilliant dance and I went to sleep out on the guards with the notes of delicious music ringing in my ears. The place is not famous for good order and decorum

---

* The run from Boonville to Brunswick was 62 miles by river; hence, the upstream speed of the *Polar Star* on this occasion was about 6 mph.

although the fame of the *"Popular" Star* was not tarnished by any belligerent demonstrations.

Wednesday, September 28th. We are now literally full, and about two ladies to one gent. Lexington, Dover, and other points turned out a generous quota of beauty. We tied up for the night a little above Glasgow.

Thursday, September 29th. This morning was a chilly, misty, sometimes rainy morning, and no indications sound very pleasant to the eye or any other of the senses. We discharged 35 bales hemp at Jefferson City, in the rain. The prisoners came down, attended by the sentinel, to cover and take care of it.

Friday, September 30th. We left a point some 15 miles above Hermann and reached St. Louis about 7 o'clock in the evening. I went back [in the cabin] and saw several ladies, Miss Porter particularly, who played and sang "The Lone, and Starry Hour," and some other home airs. She left on the *Royal Arch* for Louisville next morning.

Saturday, October 1st, 1853. Today being the first of the month which greeted my arrival in St. Louis—October 11, 1852—I have resolved to turn over a new leaf in my journal of events and proceed to carry my designs into execution. We discharged our freight consisting of 59 bales hemp, and some few other packages, and I delivered my freight with as much dispatch as possible—the weather looking decidedly low. Found letters at the post office from Aunt Arbuckle and Mary. Mailed twelve pages to Sue.

Sunday, 2d October. The day was very pleasant from the time when the skies first reddened in the East until we saw the crimson glories of the departing day. In the morning I commenced a letter to Aunt Arbuckle, which I finished after I had listened to a good sermon at the Church of Messiah and eaten heartily one of "Sol's" good dinners. Aunt writes that Mary Howard, whom she saw in Cleveland, says I am good looking, but the "general tone of her conversation concerning me was not very flattering." Perhaps the "grapes are sour." In the evening, after talking a little while to Mrs. Wilson—newly arrived from Chicago and bound for Weston—I again went up to Unitarian Church, from which I returned about 9 p.m. and immediately sought my bed.

Monday, 3rd. Small lots of freight coming down like angels visiting in this "wild wood of the West," confined me to the levee just enough to prevent engaging in any business but the one legitimate occupation. Wrote to Pa in the evening.

Tuesday, October 4th. Today we leave with a light freight and our rooms barely filled with passengers in what I judge is our last trip [on the Missouri River] of the season.

Wednesday, October 5th. Nothing of interest has passed today. The river has fallen at least a foot since our last trip. We reached Jefferson City at 8 p.m.

Friday, October 7th. As wearily as might be, we dragged our slow length along over sandbars and around snags. We reached only Camden today.

Saturday, October 8th. We were at Kansas City at noon today where we found the *St. Ange* lying with her cam broken. We were at Weston late in the evening. I saw Mrs. Riddlebarger, who was on the *Clara,* going down. I asked her how she liked Kansas City. She said, "Oh, I perfectly hate it!"

Sunday, October 9th. We arrived here [St. Joseph] about 11 o'clock in the afternoon, and I discharged my freight before dinner—although it made that exercise very late. The trip up was a slim one.

Tuesday, October 11th. We were at Weston all night and had a dance—a very decent one, except the men mostly got drunk. And in the course of the evening I was introduced to Miss E. Basey, a lady of some creditable parts.

Friday, October 14th. We did not set a spar during the trip, but we met with the best of luck and came into port with a goodly number of passengers. We reached St. Louis this evening about 6 o'clock, and Dakin, who came down with us, and myself went to the theater—or rather the opera, another name for humbug.

Saturday, October 15th. In the morning I discharged our freight, consisting principally of 55 bales hemp and 219 bundles buffalo robes which latter came on board at Kansas City.

Due to seasonal low water on the Missouri, the *Polar Star* quit the Big Muddy and made two successive trips down the Mississippi to New Orleans. On November 26, 1853, she was back in St. Louis. Her owners then decided to lay her up for winter repairs. Henry Blossom put the time to good use by enrolling in a local business college. He later gave up the river and pursued a career in the insurance field.

4

Sudden
Death

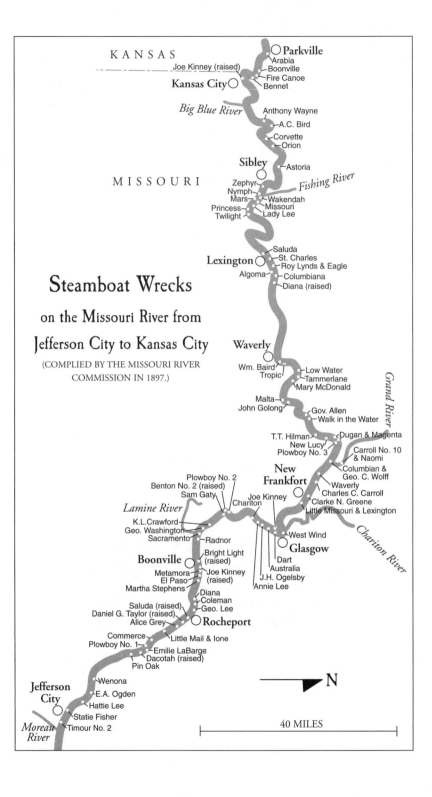

KANSAS

○ Parkville
Joe Kinney (raised) — Arabia
— Boonville
Kansas City ○ — Fire Canoe
— Bennet

Big Blue River — Anthony Wayne
— A.C. Bird
— Corvette
— Orion

Sibley — Astoria
○
MISSOURI Zephyr — *Fishing River*
Nymph —
Mars — Wakendah
Princess — Missouri
Twilight — Lady Lee

— Saluda
— St. Charles
Lexington ○ — Roy Lynds & Eagle
Algoma — Columbiana
— Diana (raised)

Steamboat Wrecks

on the Missouri River from

Jefferson City to Kansas City

(COMPLIED BY THE MISSOURI RIVER
COMMISSION IN 1897.)

Waverly
○
Wm. Baird — Low Water
Tropic — Tammerlane
— Mary McDonald

Malta —
John Golong — Gov. Allen
— Walk in the Water

Grand River

T.T. Hilman — Dugan & Magenta
New Lucy —
Plowboy No. 3 — Carroll No. 10
— & Naomi

— Columbian &
New — Geo. C. Wolff
Frankfort — Waverly
○ — Charles C. Carroll
Joe Kinney — Clarke N. Greene
Plowboy No. 2 — — Little Missouri & Lexington
Benton No. 2 (raised) — Chariton
Sam Gaty —

Lamine River

Chariton River

K.L.Crawford —
Geo. Washington — West Wind
Sacramento — Radnor —
Glasgow
○
Bright Light — Dart
Boonville ○ (raised)
Metamora — Joe Kinney — Australia
El Paso — (raised) — J.H. Ogelsby
Martha Stephens — — Annie Lee
— Diana
— Coleman
Saluda (raised) — — Geo. Lee
Daniel G. Taylor (raised) —
Alice Grey — Rocheport ○

Commerce — — Little Mail & Ione
Plowboy No. 1 —
— Emilie LaBarge
— Dacotah (raised)
Pin Oak

N

Jefferson
City — Wenona
— E.A. Ogden
○ — Hattie Lee
— Statie Fisher
Moreau — Timour No. 2
River

40 MILES

Groundings, collisions, and fires

The Missouri River claimed many a vessel. Two hundred and eighty-nine steamboats sank in the Big Muddy from 1819 through 1897. The true number probably is higher—some have put it around 400—but the lower figure was the "official" total arrived at by the Missouri River Commission.

The most frequent mishap to befall a Missouri River steamer was running aground. It was a rare trip on the Missouri when a boat did not run aground. Most of the time grounding a boat meant a delay—anywhere from an hour to several days. And when a boat got free it continued on, for seldom was there any damage. But a grounded boat *could* sink if the river bottom was uneven and the boat hard aground—the combination would cause the hull to sag and break in two. Hulls were made of heavy oaken timber, thick and rugged, but not indestructible.

Collisions with snags and rocks claimed 204 of the 289 confirmed sinkings. Those very hulls that could withstand so much grinding and scraping were surprisingly vulnerable to punctures. This was an inevitable risk of steamboating, for it was impossible to remove each snag and wreck, and deepen every shoal. Salvage companies hired by the insurers located most of the wrecks and took off as much cargo and machinery as possible. But they rarely

EXCAVATION OF THE STEAMBOAT *BERTRAND*, 1969. While steaming for Fort Benton, the *Bertrand* struck a snag and sank 20 miles north of Omaha, on April 1, 1865. The uncovered hull is shown here as it lies nearly 30 feet below ground level within the loop of DeSoto Bend. The present-day Missouri is 3,500 feet southwest of the wreckage site. The *Bertrand's* cargo is displayed in the visitors' center at DeSoto National Wildlife Refuge.
(PHOTO COURTESY DESOTO NATIONAL WILDLIFE REFUGE, U.S. FISH AND WILDLIFE SERVICE.)

got it all, and in some cases they got nothing. The wrecks remained underwater until the river changed its course, and the old bed filled with sand and silt until the wrecks were twenty or thirty feet down. And they are still there.

Collisions with other steamboats were rare—only one recorded incident on the Missouri—but they were common enough elsewhere. The worst single collision took place on the Ohio River. It occurred on December 4, 1868; sixty-three people died. The curious thing about that accident was the name of the two boats involved: the steamers *United States* and *America*.

Fires posed an ever-present danger. Twenty-five boats burned on the Missouri. Steamboat superstructures were built of pine, and covered with linseed oil-based paint; with fires in the boilers, stoves, and lights, it took only a careless moment or a hard jolt to set off a raging conflagration. One story has it that a Missouri River steamer was set on fire intentionally by would-be robbers intent on stealing money from the staterooms and safe during the confusion. But the fire got out of hand quickly, and they got nothing for their effort.

Boiler explosions

By far the deadliest risk in steamboating was the boiler explosion. Crude and imprecise methods of determining boiler water level led to most of these "burst ups." Boilers were large. A thirty-foot long boiler of forty-two inch diameter excited no great attention, for it was about average size. Most boats had two or more. Normal steam pressure within those boilers would rise to over 100 pounds per square inch. With cast iron boiler heads, loose rivets, and weak internal flues, much could go wrong. When a critical component failed there was no warning—only concussion, flame, scalding water, and searing steam. Those passengers and crew who weren't killed outright in an explosion faced the real possibility of drowning or the unthinkable horror of entombment in the rubble of a burning, sinking vessel. According to one newspaper tally, twenty-seven boiler explosions took place between 1834 and 1852 on all the Western Rivers. A total of 1,002 people were killed in these explosions.

Stories of steamboat explosions read like some kind of improbable fiction. The steamer *Big Hatchie* blew her boilers at Hermann, Missouri, on July 25, 1845. Thirty-five unidentified victims are buried in the cemetery there—where a small marker stands as a memorial. But many more bodies were thrown into the river and never recovered. To this day no one knows how many.

The steamboat *Timour* tied up at a woodyard three miles below Jefferson City, Missouri, on August 20, 1854. During the stop, some of the passengers climbed a bluff to pick wild flowers. Without any warning the *Timour's* boilers exploded and hurled debris through the air. The boat's safe came down amongst the stunned flower pickers on the bluff. They were not hurt, but nineteen persons on board, including the captain, pilot, and clerk, died in the awful discharge.

Some one hundred persons, mostly Morman emigrants, were killed in the explosion of the *Saluda*, at Lexington, Missouri, on April 9, 1852. The boat was underpowered, heavily laden, and working against a swollen river. After several attempts to negotiate a bend above the town, the captain ordered the engineer to build up steam far beyond the normal limits. When concerned passengers implored the captain to reconsider, he replied that he would "stem the current or blow her to hell." He succeeded in the latter.

This sort of erratic behavior on the part of a boat's captain happened more frequently than one might suppose. Steamboats, after all, could not make money standing still, and a boat with a reputation for speed always attracted more business. Imbued with this aggressive hell-for-leather mindset and carried away at times with the exhilaration and excitement of a record-setting run, even passengers sometimes willingly accepted the risk of an explosion. A St. Louis newspaper illustrated the point in its coverage of a race between the *Naomi* and the *Shawnee* in 1839:

> Steam was up and both boats were puffing and blowing like two alligators ready for combat. The *Naomi* was engaged to take the Grays [a militia unit] and could not go till they came, which was near 6 o'clock in the evening. The *Shawnee* held on till then, when the *Naomi* let go her fastenings, and after rounding to, passed up at a merry rate in front of the

landing; the Grays paraded, in their best uniform, making a fine appearance on the hurricane deck, and the music from the U.S. band at Jefferson Barracks which was on board, played some enlivening airs.

The *Naomi* had but just shot by the *Shawnee*, when the rival "let go all," and came on at a furious rate a few rods astern. Matters began growing interesting; and, as they dashed forward the excitement was increased by the appearance of dense smoke from the chimneys of both boats which showed that rosin or some pitchy matter was feeding the fury of the flame. There was, however, no great danger, for probably both boats conducted the race with discretion as well as spirit.

About a mile above town, at Sawyer's Bend, the *Shawnee* moved off toward the Illinois shore, while the *Naomi* hugged the curved bank on this side. At this point in the game the *Shawnee* saved a considerable distance and was quite abreast of her competitor. It would have now been an even bet on the *Shawnee*, though the odds had so far been in favor of the *Naomi*. Shortly after a mile farther ahead the *Naomi* was slightly favored by the direction of the shore, and so effecting an oblique movement she placed herself a few yards in front of the *Shawnee*. The word on both boats was "pile in your kindling stuff"; while the excitement grew to a pitch that was quite exhilarating. Both boats sprang and leaped forward, letting out all the "go" there was in them—and as they rushed onward panting and quivering it seemed for a little while somewhat uncertain which was coming out second best. The *Shawnee* had on board a very full and dragging load; the *Naomi* was in the worst possible trim. The contest did not however long remain very doubtful. Gradually symptoms of shortcoming appeared in the *Shawnee*, and finally when the Missouri River opened upon the *Naomi*, a pretty good mile separated the two boats. The race was well contested; although we believe every circumstance of danger was avoided by the extreme care taken by the engineers on both boats as to the condition of the boilers.*

This last reference to the condition of the boilers touched a nerve with many a steamboat passenger. Boilers were the heart of the steamboat, and the very things that could cause swift and cer-

---

* The *Naomi* sank in 1840 after hitting a snag at Brunswick, Missouri. Some 40 years later a farmer drilling a well near Brunswick unearthed a bible with the name *Naomi* inscribed upon it. The drilling site once had been the bed of the river and probably was over the location of the wreck.

tain destruction of the vessel. Those familiar with steam machinery aired their opinions that even racing could be made safe if the boilers were better engineered. An editorial writer in 1845 pointed out that the accepted standard of rolling boiler iron to one-quarter or five-sixteenth inch thickness was not sufficient, that one-half or five-eighths inch would be better, and that blowers could be used "to overcome the increased difficulty of generating steam in thick boilers." The same writer suggested that boilers undergo a static test of at least twice their ordinary steam pressure, and that this test ought to be repeated every four years. He opined that a boat thus tested "would be sought and waited for by passengers."

The horror of a boiler explosion always would remain in the memory of those who witnessed one, whether they were a seasoned

WRECK OF AN UNKNOWN MISSOURI RIVER STERNWHEELER.
Insurance underwriters hired salvage companies to strip everything of value from stricken vessels—including undamaged boilers and machinery. Yet, often the river tore the wrecks apart before salvors arrived at the scene.
(PHOTO COURTESY U.S. ARMY CORPS OF ENGINEERS.)

boatman or a traveler from afar. Walter B. Foster fell into the second grouping. He was a young man who had journeyed by sea from his home in Portland, Maine, to New Orleans. From there he booked passage on a riverboat to St. Louis. The trip was uneventful. He had but one more leg to his travels, for he planned to proceed to Glasgow, Missouri, where he had secured a teaching appointment. He kept a dairy of his trip in order that he might remember the incidents of his great excursion. The events of one fateful day, though, would overshadow all that had come before. He shuddered as he wrote:

On Saturday, the 2d of July [1842] went on board steamboat *Iatan* bound from St. Louis up Missouri River. We ran up to the mouth of the Missouri that night where we laid by, as is customary for boats in this trade on account of the dangers of navigation in the night. In the course of the night the *Edna* came up and laid alongside. Both boats got up steam at daylight on the morning of the 3d but whether from a wish to race or from some other cause, the *Edna,* who laid outside us, did not seem inclined to put out. The *Iatan* therefore dropped astern and ran past the *Edna* about a quarter past four o'clock. I was asleep at the time of dropping astern but was awake when the machinery was put in motion. I looked out my stateroom window as we passed and then laid down again, but had scarcely done so when I heard a crash followed by shouts. Our machinery was instantly stopped and our clerk, running aft, called out that the *Edna* had blown up, and upon listening I could hear the cries of the wounded softened by the distance as they were borne over the water on the still morning air.

I dressed and went on deck and in a few minutes we were alongside. The scene that here met our eyes no person can describe. The *Edna* had nearly one hundred deck passengers and nearly all of these were either killed or wounded. The shrieks and groans from the disabled boat were horrid beyond all description. I went on board to assist in taking care of the wounded—the scene that presented itself I shall never forget.

The entire deck aft of the boilers was a complete wreck. The dead, wounded, and dying were scattered in all directions—some lying upon one another, others half-buried in the goods and rubbish blown in piles by the explosion, while screams and prayers, curses and groans, resounded from all sides.

"Water! Water!! Water!!!" was the cry in all directions. Poor fellows, they were burning with thirst and imagined no one cared for their sufferings. Some begged in the most piteous accents to be killed at once, some uttered shriek upon shriek in the most heart-rending manner, while others lay perfectly silent, but the frightening manner in which they would look up in our eyes was ever more afflicting than cries.

One could scarce move without touching the dead, dying, or wounded. Some imagined they were freezing while others thought themselves burning to death and their cries were alike horrible.

A part of the wounded were removed on board the *Iatan* and a part were placed in the cabin of the *Edna*. The latter boat was taken in tow by the *Annawan,* which very fortunately just then came down the Mississippi. The three boats then proceeded to St. Louis.

Our cabin and social hall were crowded fore and aft with the wounded. The mattresses and blankets of the boats were taken out, the wounded placed upon them and an attempt made to keep them covered with clothes, but the slightest touch was so painful to them that it was utterly impossible to keep many of them from tearing off the blankets placed on them. Fortunately we had a case of linseed oil upon our boiler deck and with this we bathed the sufferers and which, although it seemed scarcely to afford them any relief, was undoubtedly the best remedy that could be applied. On the arrival of the boat at St. Louis the surgeons came on board and dressed the wounds with sweet oil and cotton, and the unfortunate sufferers were then removed to the hospital.

One very respectable looking man, who called his name Henly, from Montgomery County, first struck my attention. He seemed very pale but lay perfectly quiet uttering no complaint. I asked him if he would have a glass of wine and water, he assented. Upon inquiring I found that his hand had been blown in pieces in the explosion, and upon further examination at St. Louis it was ascertained that his arm was broken in two places. His head was badly cut and he was somewhat scalded. Yet he seemed perfectly conscious of everything that had taken place. He told me that he was standing upon the forecastle of the boat at the same time of the accident. [He] was struck by some fragments, blown over the bow, and came up under the boat. When his head struck the boat's bottom he sank again and, being borne along by the current, finally came up astern and got first on the shore and then on the boat.

Another, a young man bearing my own name, was horribly scalded. I assisted in cutting off his clothes. He suffered twenty deaths and yet in the midst of his agony he could not help thinking of the horrid appear-

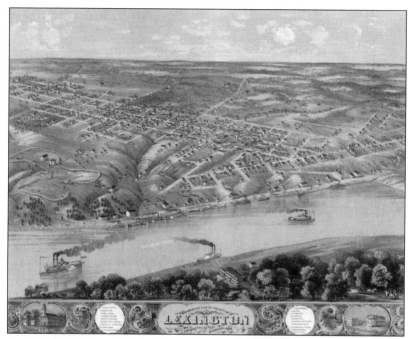

BIRDSEYE VIEW OF LEXINGTON, MISSOURI, 1869. Located in the hemp growing region of the lower valley, Lexington was the site of the *Saluda* disaster. Several children orphaned by the explosion were adopted by families in Lexington. The Civil War breastworks on the bluffs overlooking the river (middle left) are now are part of the Battle of Lexington State Historic Site.
(COURTESY LIBRARY OF CONGRESS.)

ance he must make if he recovered. His first exclamation was, "Oh, God! My friends wouldn't know me!"

A young German woman who was badly scalded nearly over her whole person begged of me to cut the skin which had been taken from her arms and hands like a glove and was hanging by the nails. I accordingly obtained a razor [and] did as she desired.

Several children aged twelve to fifteen years were literally flayed alive; there was not a particle of skin upon their bodies. Some lay insensible and made no noise; others kept screaming. One very strong man aged about 35 was very badly scalded and I judged had inhaled steam. Another man about the same age, a German and a perfect giant in appearance, was likewise horribly scalded, so much that [on] his face, where the boiling water seemed to have struck with most force, the blood had stagnated. He also had inhaled the steam and the shrieks of these two men seemed to drown all the rest.

One little child died on our boat on the passage down. He was one of a large family of German emigrants, all of whom were so badly scalded as to probably cause death. They lay side by side: the father, mother, and nine children, some of them grown young women. When the little child died, the mother raised her head for a moment and looked at it and then sunk back again upon the mattress. Could she have reasoned as I did, she would not certainly have regretted its death.

Even in the midst of all this suffering, some of the passengers of both boats who had escaped unhurt seemed to be perfectly indifferent to the distress and misery around them. Some drank, some smoked and laughed, others endeavored to keep as far from the horrible sights and sounds as possible. Some devoted their whole attention to the sufferers and seemed ready and willing to do everything for them while others again seemed perfectly astounded by the scene around them and incapable of attending to anything.

On board the *Edna* a German who had been killed was stripped of his clothes and a belt of savings found upon him. An Irishman standing by pocketed it, but was afterwards forced to give it up. Strange that in a scene like this one could be so depraved! But enough—

At least 43 people died in the explosion of the *Edna*. One newspaper account put the number as high as 65. Most of those killed were immigrant deck passengers. On July 4, more than a thousand people in St. Louis attended a public funeral for the victims.

Epidemic disease

The perils of steamboat passage knew no bounds—especially for deck passengers. If not dismembered in an explosion, or scalded by a broken steam pipe, deck passengers might expect to be burned in a fire, or trapped among debris on a sinking vessel. And, too, they might fall victim to yet another scourge that betimes ravaged their kind. While splendidly isolated cabin passengers up on the boiler deck stuffed themselves at mealtime and chatted pleasantly around the heating stove, the passengers below may have been facing a nightmare of devastating proportions. Two St. Louis newspaper articles, dated May 5 and 8, 1849 spell out the demon:

> CHOLERA. Eleven deaths on the steamer *St. Paul* [have taken place] on her passage up the Missouri River, and rumors are rife in relation to the appearance and mortality of this frightful disease on several other steamers now on the way up, the extent of which is no doubt much exaggerated. It is reported that four deaths took place on the steamer *Algona* between this place and Wayne City.
>
> * * * * * * * * *
>
> GREAT MORTALITY. The officers of the steamer *St. Joseph,* down yesterday from Council Bluffs, reported having met the steamer *Mary* at Glasgow, bound up, with a number of Morman emigrants on board. Captain Scott, of the *Mary,* informed the officers of the *St. Joseph* that there had been twenty-one deaths on board since she left this city; four corpses were still on board, and there were ten or twelve down with the same disease—cholera. The mortality was confined solely to the Morman emigrants on deck, a great many of whom reached this city a few days previous from New Orleans, in the worst possible condition as regards health.

The *Mary* continued upriver with her death toll continually rising. By the time she reached Lexington thirty of her deck passengers had died; five more died before she reached Fort Leavenworth. News of the deadly journey preceded her. When she hove into view at St. Joseph, the town authorities were on hand to wave her off. She had to land on the opposite bank to discharge freight. Forty-seven of her original 350-plus passengers were now dead. Most of the deceased were buried in makeshift graves along the river, graves that would wash away in the next high water. The *Mary* turned around after leaving the St. Joe area and stood downriver for St. Louis. By the time she arrived there a total of fifty-six passengers had died—all deck passengers.

Captain Scott and his crew obviously were men of good character. They had risked their own lives in taking the surviving passengers back to St. Louis. In so doing they had passed the steamer *James Monroe,* which was tied to the bank about a mile below Jefferson City. Cholera had claimed at least thirty-seven deck passengers on the *Monroe,* but in marked contrast to the brave crew of the *Mary,* the officers and crew of the *Monroe* had abandoned the vessel and left the stricken passengers to their fate.

By July the cholera had reached epidemic proportions in St. Louis. The disease had gotten its start amidst the filth and unsanitary conditions of deck passage on boats arriving from New Orleans, and in like manner was carried up the Missouri. Further outbreak could be checked only by strict quarantine measures. To this end, the city council of St. Louis established a quarantine station on an island in front of the city. Any boat arriving with infected passengers had to land her passengers at the station. A chartered steamboat was moored there to serve as a hospital receiving vessel. No one could leave quarantine until all new cases had abated. Within a month it was over, but not before some 4,500 deaths had occurred in the city.

5

Up the
Wild Missouri

FORT BENTON, MONTANA TERRITORY, 1880. Though more than a hundred miles from the gold fields of southwest Montana, Fort Benton was the head of steamboat navigation on the Missouri River and the closest transfer point for travelers and goods going to and from the mining camps. The vessel in the lower foreground is a rope ferry crossing the river. A sternwheeler lies moored to the shore in the distant background.

Westward bound

St. Louis was the great inland port of the United States, a teeming gateway city of 60,000-plus permanent inhabitants. The city was a funnel to the West, and the highway of preference was the Missouri River. St. Louis was a cosmopolitan city—not simply as a result of its French heritage, but rather more because of the influx of people moving west. This same variegated and eclectic mix of humankind was found on every boat that cleared St. Louis for the Missouri River.* Father Pierre-Jean DeSmet caught the essence of it in a letter-journal he kept of his 1840 trip upriver:

> The craft on which I had embarked was (like all of them in this land, where emigration and commerce have grown to such an extent) encumbered with freight and passengers from every state of the Union; I may even say from the various nations of the earth: white, black, yellow, and red, with shadings of all these colors. The boat was like a little floating Babel, on account of the different languages and jargons that were heard upon it. These passengers drop off here and there on the river, to open farms, construct mills, build factories of every kind; they increase day by day the number of the inhabitants of the little towns and villages that spring up as if by magic, on both sides of the river.

---

* It typically was a three-hour steamboat ride on the Mississippi River from the St. Louis wharf to the mouth of the Missouri, but for all practical purposes a trip on the Missouri began and ended at St. Louis.

A sense of excitement always accompanied a trip up the Missouri. The adventure, the danger, the sheer immensity of the West—it all began the moment the lines were cast loose and the boat backed out into the channel. One could hardly know what to expect. The famed ornithologist John James Audubon knew the exhilaration of it. He arranged passage up the Missouri aboard the *Omega* in order to gain first-hand knowledge of winged creatures of the far country. The *Omega* was chartered to the American Fur Company, which sent a boat high up the Missouri each year. Audubon kept a journal, and he described the scene as the vessel prepared to leave St. Louis on April 23, 1843:

> First the general embarkation, when the men came in pushing and squeezing each other, so as to make the boards they walked fairly tremble. The Indians, poor souls, were more quiet, and had already seated or squatted themselves on the highest parts of the steamer, and were tranquil lookers-on. After about three-quarters of an hour, the crew and all the trappers (these are called *engages*) were on board, and we at once pushed off and up the stream, thick and muddy as it was. The whole of the effects and the baggage of the *engages* was arranged in the main cabin, and presently was seen Mr. [John B.] Sarpy [a partner in the company], book in hand, with the list before him. The men whose names were called filled the fore part of the cabin, where stood Mr. Sarpy, our captain, and one of the clerks. As each man was called, and answered to his name, a blanket containing the apparel for the trip was handed to him, and he was ordered at once to retire and make room for the next. The outfit, by the way, was somewhat scanty, and of indifferent quality. Four men were missing, and some appeared rather reluctant; however, the roll was ended, and one hundred and one were found. In many instances their bundles were thrown to them, and they were ordered off as if slaves.
>
> I forgot to say that as the boat pushed off from the shore, where stood a crowd of loafers, the men on board had congregated upon the hurricane deck with their rifles and guns of various sorts, all loaded, and began to fire what I should call a very disorganized sort of salute, which lasted for something like an hour, and which has been renewed at intervals, though in a more desultory manner, at every village as we passed. We now find them passably good, quiet, and regularly sobered men.

The *engagés* aboard the *Omega* were contract employees of the fur company. They would spend a year or more in the mountains before returning home. For many others a trip up the Missouri was the first leg of a transcontinental migration from which they had no intention of returning. From the shores of the Big Muddy great westward trails meandered across the prairies and mountains to Santa Fe, California, Utah, and Oregon. One of the thousands to make the trip was one Francis Parkman, a young adventurer from New England. He journeyed westward from St. Louis in 1846 and later published his memoirs as the classic work, *The California and Oregon Trail.* His voyage from St. Louis to the future site of Kansas City was typical of the times:

> Almost every day steamboats were leaving the levee and passing up the Missouri, crowded with passengers on their way to the frontier. In one of these, the *Radnor,* since snagged and lost, my friend and relative, Quincy A. Shaw, and myself, left St. Louis on the twenty-eighth of April, on a tour of curiosity and amusement to the Rocky Mountains. The boat was loaded until the water broke alternately over her guards. Her upper deck was covered with large wagons of a peculiar form, for the Santa Fe trade, and her hold was crammed with goods for the same destination. There were also equipments and provisions of a party of Oregon emigrants, a band of mules and horses, piles of saddles and harness, and a multitude of nondescript articles, indispensable on the prairies. Almost hidden in this medley one might have seen a small French cart, of the sort very appropriately called a "mule-killer" beyond the frontiers, and not far distant a tent, together with a miscellaneous assortment of boxes and barrels. The whole equipage was far from prepossessing in its appearance; yet, such as it was, it was destined to a long and arduous journey.
>
> The passengers on board the *Radnor* corresponded with her freight. In her cabin were Santa Fe traders, gamblers, speculators, and adventurers of various descriptions, and her steerage was crowded with Oregon emigrants, "mountain men," Negroes, and a party of Kanza Indians, who had been on a visit to St. Louis.
>
> Thus laden, the boat struggled upward for seven or eight days against the rapid current of the Missouri, grating upon snags, and hanging for two or three hours at a time upon sandbars. We entered the mouth of the

Missouri in a drizzling rain, but the weather soon became clear, and showed distinctly the broad and turbid river, with its eddies, its sandbars, its ragged islands and forest-covered shores. The Missouri is constantly changing its course; wearing away its banks on one side, while it forms new ones on the other. Its channel is shifting continually. Islands are formed, and then washed away; and while the old forests on one side are undermined and swept off, a young growth springs up from the new soil upon the other. With all these changes, the water is so charged with mud and sand that it is perfectly opaque, and in a few minutes deposits a sediment an inch thick in the bottom of a tumbler. The river was now high; but when we descended in the autumn it was fallen very low, and all the secrets of its treacherous shallows were exposed to view. It was frightful to see the dead and broken trees, thick-set as a military abattis, firmly imbedded in the sand, and all pointing downstream, ready to impale any unhappy steamboat that at high water should pass over that dangerous ground.

In five or six days we began to see signs of the great western movement that was then taking place. Parties of emigrants, with their tents and wagons, would be encamped on open spots near the bank, on their way to the common rendezvous at Independence. On a rainy day, near sunset, we reached the landing of this place, which is situated some miles from the river, on the extreme frontier of Missouri. The scene was characteristic, for here were represented at one view the most remarkable features of this wild and enterprising region. On the muddy shore stood some thirty or forty dark slavish-looking Spaniards, gazing stupidly out from beneath their broad hats. They were attached to one of the Santa Fe companies, whose wagons were crowded together on the banks above. In the midst of these, crouching over a smoldering fire, was a group of Indians, belonging to a remote Mexican tribe. One or two French hunters from the mountains, with their long hair and buckskin dresses, were looking at the boat; and seated on a log close at hand were three men, with rifles lying across their knees. The foremost of these, a tall, strong figure, with a clear blue eye and an open, intelligent face, might very well represent that race of restless and intrepid pioneers whose axes and rifles have opened a path from the Alleghenies to the western prairies. He was on his way to Oregon, probably a more congenial field to him than any that now remained on this side of the great plains.

Early on the next morning we reached Kanzas, about five hundred miles from the mouth of the Missouri. Here we landed, and leaving our equipments in charge of my good friend Colonel Chick, . . . we set out in a wagon for Westport, where we hoped to procure mules and horses for the journey.

From St. Louis to the Dakotas

Every fan of the book *Life on the Mississippi* knows that Mark Twain's chief, Horace Ezra Bixby, left the lower valley for a time to try his hand at Missouri River piloting. Although Mr. Bixby applied himself wholeheartedly to the task, he did not attain the level of success that he enjoyed on the Mississippi. In 1866, as captain and first pilot of the steamer *Rubicon,* Bixby failed to make his intended destination of Fort Benton, in Montana territory, and turned around at Milk River, 350 miles below. It was Bixby's only try at the mountains; he left the Missouri a humbled man. Many years later, when Bixby was 83 and possibly the oldest and most respected active Mississippi riverman, he commented about the pilots who spent their careers on the Missouri. "Any man," he said, "who can run a boat for twenty years in that rainwater creek above Bismarck is surely the king of pilots."

Successful pilots on the Upper Missouri possessed rare talents. Owing to the short season, they ran the river only once or twice per year, and it never presented the same channel to them. Certainly they were a boastful lot; after all, they took their vessels up to the mountains where steamboats were never intended to go. And yet their boasts were not without merit, for there was something peculiar about the Missouri—something that warranted the quadrupling of a Mississippi pilot's pay; something that set boat builders to designing "spoonbill" bows and "bustle" sterns; something that compelled rivermen to risk everything through two thousand miles of the highest winds, lowest water, deadliest Indians, and most numerous snags of any river on the continent. The Missouri was a Western stream in the true sense: a river that flowed not only along the frontier, but beyond it. In summing up the difficulties, one pilot put it this way: "We used to separate the

STEAMBOAT *GENERAL TERRY* AT FORT BERTHOLD (NORTH DAKOTA) IN 1880. Note the well-rounded spoonbill bow that allowed the pilot to beach the boat at shallow landings without the use of mooring lines— a necessity on the treeless reaches of the upper river. The *General Terry* ran on both the Missouri and Yellowstone Rivers and once carried a load of 10,000 buffalo hides that covered all but her pilothouse.

(PHOTO COURTESY HAYES FOUNDATION COLLECTION
MONTANA HISTORICAL SOCIETY.)

men from the boys at the mouth of the Missouri. The boys went up the Mississippi and the men up the Big Muddy."

Could it really have been that bad? The best way to find out is to take a trip up there. We have two good accounts of upward journeys. The first is from the log of the steamer *Omega*. She is captained by Joseph A. Sire and piloted by Joseph LaBarge. This is the trip that included John J. Audubon as a passenger. We will ride as far as Fort Pierre, near the middle of what is today the state of South Dakota. The log, extracted here, originally was written in French, probably by Captain Sire:

> April 25 [1843]. Tuesday. Left St. Louis at 11 a.m. Water high but falling slightly. Current strong. We make slow progress. Reach St. Charles at 4 o'clock next morning. . . .

> April 26. Wednesday. Set out at 6 a.m. Current still strong. Took wood twice. The river is undoubtedly in fine condition for night running; but it is dark and the weather threatening. Moreover, we have too much to lose to risk our cargo for the sake of gaining a little time.

> April 28. Friday. The current still strong and the river rising. Wooded at 11 a.m., nine miles above Jefferson City. Much difficulty in finding wood. We found some by chance, 4½ cords, below the large island four miles below Rocheport. We tried in vain to stem the current along the bluffs. At 10 p.m. I decided to put to shore on a little island in order not to consume our wood to no purpose.

> April 30. Sunday. Set out at 4 a.m. Current still strong, and to cap the climax the wind rises with incredible force. It is useless to try to keep on, and we put to shore four miles from our last camp where, most fortunately, we find poles and dry mulberry, which permits us to fill the boat. At 1 p.m. the wind seems to moderate. We set out, and thanks to the wood which we had chopped and the poles we had taken, we get along very well. As the night is fine we continue our voyage....Passed Lexington at the dinner hour, where we were overtaken by the *John Auld*, which passed along by.

> May 2. Tuesday. Set out before day. It seems that we are making better progress. In fact, since the water is falling the current is less strong. Passed the bad place at the mouth of the Kansas River after sunset. The

weather was so fine that I decided to run all night. At 6 a.m. we reached Leavenworth.

May 3. Wednesday. Set out at 8 a.m. We got along well, although often slowly. At 4 p.m. we reached the little island below village 24. In order to avoid a bad chute on the right we took the left-hand channel and had the misfortune to run aground. We got ourselves clear once, but had the misfortune to get fast crosswise the channel. It rained and blew in a frightful manner. We were compelled to stay where we were for the night in the hope of extricating ourselves in the morning.

May 4. Thursday. We get clear, but by a false maneuver of the pilot we get aground again. Broke our large cable. Finally succeeded in getting off by shoving the stern around. The wind blows with incredible force, and we have to pass a place very dangerous on account of snags.

May 6. Saturday. The wind blows frightfully all night, with such violence that it seems as though the smokestacks would be blown down. It moderates a little at sunrise and we set out. We do not go far before it blows as strong as it did before. It is one o'clock before we resume our journey, and in spite of wind and current we arrive at the Iowas at sunset, where I discharge the freight for the agent.

May 10. Wednesday. We progressed finely as far as Hart's Bluffs, where we were summoned by an [Army] officer and four dragoons to land. I received a polite note from Captain Burgwin, informing me that his duty obliged him to make an inspection of the boat [for contraband whiskey]. We put ourselves to work immediately [hiding the whiskey], while Mr. Audubon goes to call upon the captain. They return in about two hours. I compel, as it were, the officer to make the strictest possible inspection, but on the condition that he would do the same with other traders. Resumed our journey at noon.

May 12. Friday. Scarcely had we started when we were obliged to lay to on account of the fog. Started again half an hour later. Found the difficult chute of the Little River of the Sioux stopped up, and the channel passing through the mud bars.

May 15. Monday. The wind continues to blow as hard as yesterday. I set the men to cutting driftwood again. At about 3 p.m. the wind seems to soften. We set out, but Great Heaven, how slow we go! Often we drift backward by the force of the current. We come as far as to the foot of the bluffs of the Little Iowa River. Last night the river rose 14 inches, and I think that it is still rising. The *Omega* does all she can, but she is too heavily loaded to continue against a strong current like this, and the wind of this country, which is almost always strong.

May 16. Tuesday. The river rose 11 inches last night, and consequently we have a hell of a current. It is 11:30 a.m. when we reach the Vermillion houses. We set out again at 12:30, after having taken on some wood which I left there last year; but scarcely had we doubled the point of the island when the engineer announced the sad news that one of our boilers had burned out. We have to tie up, and I much fear that we shall be here a part of tomorrow.

May 18. Thursday. It takes us another day to complete our repairs. This is due to the difficulty of introducing rivets between the flues and the wall of the boiler. The water continues to fall rapidly—three feet since yesterday noon.

May 22. Monday. We push out at 3 a.m. All along the bluffs, where it is shallow, we move slowly. Cut more wood at 6 a.m., some miles below Handy's. It is necessary to take wood whenever one can find it. In passing Handy's point a party of savages fired a volley at us, two shots of which passed through the men's cabin. Fortunately no one was hit. It is probably those rascally Santees; no one else would be capable of such an attack.*

May 23. Tuesday. After cutting some wood we set out at 5:30 a.m. Took on board the hunters whom I sent out last night. Passed the Three Islands safely, but opposite Bijoux Hills at Desire Island I plunge into the sandbars and soon we are aground athwart the current. Our spars break and it is dark before Durack returns with others. We will begin again tomorrow morning. The heat has been unsupportable all day. Thermometer 92 degrees.

---

* Audubon mentions this same attack in his journal:

"Observed some seven or eight Indians looking at us, and again retiring to the woods, as if to cover themselves; when we came nearly opposite them, however, they all came to the shore, and made signs to induce us to land. The boat did not stop for their pleasure, and after we had fairly passed them they began firing at us, not with blank cartridges, but with well-directed rifle-balls, several of which struck the *Omega* in different places.

"I was standing at that moment by one of the chimneys, and saw a ball strike the water a few feet beyond our bows; and Michaux, the hunter, heard its passing within a few inches of his head. A Scotchman, who was asleep below, was awakened and greatly frightened by hearing a ball pass through the partition, cutting the lower part of his pantaloons, and deadening itself against a trunk. . . . It seems to me a wonder that not one person was injured, standing on deck as we were to the number of a hundred or more."

May 24. Wednesday. We find the boat in the morning pretty much in the same situation. We set at work immediately and are just about to get afloat again when one of the spars break, and we are obliged to send two miles to look for another on an island where they are very scarce. It is 10 a.m. and the yawl has not returned. The yawl returns at last and we succeed in extricating ourselves, but we go aground again, again get off, and after having sounded again find only one passage and that a doubtful one. We lurch and break one of our rudders, but 10 minutes afterward we are afloat. We put to shore to mend the rudder, and meanwhile I have some wood cut from drift.

May 26. Friday. We are a little late in starting, for it is very necessary to see clearly before leaving the channel. Sent out the yawl. Found the same depth again, four feet four inches. Passed through. Stopped at the foot of the bluffs below Fort Lookout, where we cut more cedar, which we have to go a good way for. We had much trouble at two places in passing Fort Lookout point. We passed to the right of Deslaurier's Island for the first time. Much trouble in passing along the bluffs below the Great Bend. Put ashore Mr. Audubon, his companions, and three men, who will camp on the other side of the Bend and wait for us there.

May 27. Saturday. Scarcely have we set out when we consumed two hours making a crossing. A little farther it looks for a moment as if we should be obliged to lighten the cargo a half (it was raining in torrents), but we have the good luck to get through. Passed the chain of rocks at dinner time, and at 3 p.m. arrived at the head of the Great Bend, where I have some wood cut, and Mr. Audubon and companions return on board.

May 31. Wednesday. It seems that we may not be able to reach [Fort Pierre], for we shall not be able to pass along the small island below the fort. We resolve to try the small channel to the left, but after a long trail we are convinced that it is impossible. I send to the fort for the ferry boat and a Mackinaw boat, and having transferred some lead and tobacco we are able to pass up the right of the island. We reach the fort at 3 p.m. The unloading of the freight for this post is finished at sundown.

The *Omega* continued on to Fort Union, on the present-day Montana border. Along the way the search for wood became as critical as the hunt for open channels. She made it, though, reaching Fort Union on June 12. After only one day's layover to make repairs, *Omega* started down the river. It was just the same: high winds, scarce wood, and a bad channel. But running with the current and with the wind at her stern, the *Omega* fairly flew downriver. She reached St. Louis in the near record time of 15 days.

The log of the Lillie Martin

The second trip log takes us up the Missouri some 23 years later. One would expect some improvements in the interim. We shall see. We ride the *Lillie Martin,* a two-year-old sternwheeler that measures 159 feet long, with a 33-foot beam, and a draft of four feet. She is bound for the mouth of the Marias River, the lower landing for Fort Benton, a trifle over 2,600 miles from St. Louis. She has a barge lashed alongside as a lighter. The year is 1865:

> Steamer *Lillie Martin* left St. Louis, Thursday, April 6th, at 4 o'clock p.m.; lay all night at Madison Coal Yard, on account of wind, and also to have some alterations made about the rudder.
>
> Friday, April 7th. Wind blowing into shore had some difficulty in getting out. Left about 6 o'clock a.m. Wind continued to blow all day.
>
> Tuesday, April 11th. Left at 5 o'clock a.m. Weather cool and cloudy. Passed *Silver Lake* aground at Hill's Landing. Also passed *Jennie Lewis* and *Mollie Dozier,* both aground at Mathew's—the *Mollie Dozier* with her rudder broken. Lay all night at Camden.
>
> Wednesday, April 12th. Left Camden at 5 o'clock a.m. Lay all night at Kansas City; here some of our crew jumped.
>
> Monday, April 17th. This morning had to lay still on account of wind. Here some of the passengers amused themselves by hunting. About 2 o'clock wind lulled; started out, met steamer *Kate Kinney.* The wind increased so as to cause us to lay up at head of Squaw Point Bend.
>
> Wednesday, April 19th. Left at daylight. Tied up above Peru to sound. Channel played out. While here wind raised. Started out about dusk, wind increased. Drifted down below the town of Peru and anchored.

Thursday, April 20th. Left at daylight. Lay...on a bar all day at Line Island. Got off about dark, and then got on another sandbar where we lay all night.

Friday, April 21st. Got off bar at 2 o'clock p.m. after working hard all the time sparring, etc. Here it rained, sleeted, and snowed and turned very cold. Lay all night 4 miles above Otto, in company with steamer *Sam Gaty*. Night dark and cold.

Saturday, April 22. Got off at 8 o'clock a.m., being detained in cleaning boilers. Arrived at Nebraska City at 10 o'clock a.m. Here it blew a perfect gale, making it difficult to get to the landing. Was compelled to stay here until the wind lulled, which was about 4 o'clock p.m. Started again and laid up below Rockport.

Thursday, April 27th. Left at daylight, river low; some difficulty in finding channel. About 10 o'clock picked up a snag on the starboard bow, just in the powder magazine, which caused us to lay up to a sandbar and repair.

Saturday, April 29th. Left early this morning and made a good day's trip considering we fought with sandbars. Saw many Indians today. Landed at Blackbird Mission and wooded. Here we found wood higher than at any place along the river.

Monday, May 1st. Left at daylight. Wind high and very cold. About 9 o'clock [wind] raised so much that we were compelled to lay up. Started at 4 o'clock, and after making slow progress and butting bars, finally came to a halt where we lay all night below LaPlant's woodyard.

Wednesday, May 3. We lay here, wind bound, all day. While here, put in a new rudder; also passengers and crew cut about 8 cords wood.

Thursday, May 4th. Left this morning about daylight, had a tolerable good day's run. Got aground about 3 o'clock where we had some trouble in sparring; finally got off. While lying aground 25 canoes of Indians of the Winnebago tribe went down. Weather pleasant and warm; it is the first day like summer since we left. Lay all night below Vermillion.

Thursday, May 18th. Still tied up waiting for water. Weather clear and pleasant. At dark made up mind to lighten. The *Twilight* dropped down and also lightened.

Friday, May 19th. At daylight found the river on the rise, sufficient to reload, which kept us until late, so that we were not far from the same neighborhood at dark.

Saturday, May 20th. Left at daylight and made a fair day's run. This day we lost a beautiful little child of Judge Bruce of St. Joe, it having died of measles.

Monday, May 22. Started early this day, and made a good day's run. Landed at Crow Creek Agency about 11 o'clock to leave the remains of the little child who died on Saturday. Was detained but short time. Made a good run this evening, but just at dark got on a bar. But this being the first for a day or two, we could afford not to grumble.

Tuesday, May 23. Left at daylight this morning. About breakfast time found low water and had to sound. Succeeded in getting over, and made a good run until 3 o'clock, where we got aground and had to spar until sunset, when succeeded in getting over, and ran until we got about 5 miles above Medicine River, and lay all night cutting wood.

Thursday, May 25th. After raining all night, the day broke clear and pleasant. Here we were detained in delivering our goods for Ft. Sully. Tonight is the first in some time that we have not had the company of the steamer *Twilight*, she having got ahead while we were detained in delivering goods.

Friday, May 26th. Started this morning at daylight. After catching up with the *Twilight* ran about 5 miles when we found the water very low. After getting over for ourselves, had to wait and assist the *Twilight*, in which we had made an agreement to stay with each other. This we think an advantage to both. We lent the *Twilight* our barge and also our yawl to remove her freight which she had started to lighten up with. By this means she accomplished in a day what would take her 5 days to do.

Tuesday, May 30th. River continues to be in a good stage. Lay all night in company with *Twilight* where some of our passengers attended a funeral service of one of the *Twilight's* passengers. It was a solemn affair, it being at nightfall. Lay all night above Soldier Village.

Wednesday, May 31st. Today we left at daylight and made a fair day's run, considering that we had to cut wood twice. Weather clear and warm. River in the rise. Arrived at Ft. Rice about 7 o'clock. Here we had to report a list of passengers and freight.* Lay all night at the fort.

---

* The Civil War was in its final days and the Federal government required all passengers proceeding upriver to take an oath of allegiance.

Thursday, June 1st. Left this morning at 3 o'clock a.m. Run until 7 o'clock when we had to wood. Learned that the Indians were very troublesome, so it made our hunters very careful, and this made our game rather scarce. Today two of our passengers had a little set to which resulted in no one being hurt.

Friday, June 2d. Left this morning as usual early and run until about 9 o'clock when we laid up to wood. Here the wind increased so that we were compelled to lay all day, until 6 o'clock p.m. The *Twilight* tried three times until 4 o'clock p.m. to pass the point, but could not succeed. We offered to pass the point and assist her, but she finally succeeded. Ran about 5 miles where we both lay all night.

Tuesday, June 6th. Left this morning at the usual time, and made a fair day's run. Had to wood twice during the day. At about 5 o'clock saw buffalo on shore and in the river. Tried to get them but could not. At dark lay up about 50 miles above Ft. Berthold. While here, the steamer *Yellowstone* arrived from above and lay all night alongside. Everybody was preparing letters to forward, as such an opportunity does not offer often.

Wednesday, June 7th. Started this morning at 3 o'clock. Weather clear and warm. River still continues to rise, today very rapid. Had to wood 3 times during the day. At nightfall killed 4 buffalo. Had some excitement and considerable sport in getting them aboard, as they were killed in the river. Lay about 75 miles above Ft. Berthold.

Thursday, June 8th. Left this morning about daylight and run until 9 o'clock when we had to wood. Ran again until dinner time, when our machinery got out of order and we were detained until 5 o'clock when we got off. Today we saw the grandest sight of the season: buffalo by the thousands. We also caught a calf which we designed to carry to St. Louis.

Thursday, June 15th. Left this morning at daylight. At 8 o'clock this morning found the river in a very bad condition; was detained until noon in sounding. After finding the channel, started ahead and was from 12 until 2 o'clock in getting over. Ran until 6 o'clock when stopped to wood. After getting our supply, started and moved up about one mile to an open prairie, it being considered safer than the place we were wooding at, as we were in Indian country. River falling and in bad condition. Lay all night about 10 miles above the mouth of Milk River.

Tuesday, June 20. Left this morning at 4 o'clock a.m. Run until 5 o'clock a.m. when we met the *St. John* and *Effie Deans*. Here we stopped one hour in putting letters aboard and receiving passengers who had come to meet their families. Wooded during the day 3 times. Lay up at 8 o'clock p.m. where we made a good addition to our wood pile. Weather clear and pleasant. River stationary. Lay all night 10 miles below Two Calf Island.

Thursday, June 22d. Last night in the wind the *Twilight* got badly aground and today we commenced at 4 o'clock a.m. in making preparations to lighten her off. After discharging part of our freight, went to her assistance and lightened her so that she was able to get off and thereby was saved from breaking in two. Finished in getting through at 6 o'clock p.m. Started ahead again but went but a little way when stopped to find channel. Here we came to the conclusion to lighten up, and put off enough so that we can make an attempt to go ahead.

Saturday, June 24th. Left this morning at daylight, and made very fair headway. Wooded twice during the day. Found the river becoming more narrow and water very strong. Succeeded in getting along until we rounded Daufin's Rapids, having arrived there at 4 o'clock p.m. Here the *Twilight* tried to make the ripple but could not. Afterwards we tried and met with the same success. Opinions varied as to our ability to get over.

Sunday, June 25th. This morning at daylight tried to get over Daufin's Rapids, but failed. Had to drop back and lighten. This took us until dinner time. After dinner the passengers (excepting ladies) all went ashore, and spent the afternoon there, awaiting the *Lillie's* getting over. After a lengthy trial she failed, the hawser having broken which caused her to drop back very fast, and gave those who remained aboard a good fright. After the dropping she landed on the bar, and remained all night. Here the passengers who were ashore were ferried over to the boat and had to wade some distance in the water before getting on board. This created a good deal of amusement to those who were lucky enough to have remained aboard.

Monday, June 26th. Still at Daufin's Rapids. Started at 6 o'clock to try again and see if we can get over. After some time and constant perseverance we finally succeeded in getting over, which caused great rejoicing. The balance of the day was consumed in reloading the freight lightened.

Thursday, June 29th. This morning we made an early start, and everyone seemed pleased and busy in preparing to commence overland trip by the way of a change. We stopped to wood several times, and at 1 o'clock arrived in sight of mouth of Marias. Here we fired a salute, as this was to be our journey's end. After arranging preliminaries com-

menced discharging freight. Here we also received a big lot of passengers
for the down trip; these with the up passengers made us quite crowded.
Tomorrow our up passengers leave us. Weather clear and pleasant.

The down bound trip of the *Lillie Martin* was no easier than
the voyage up. It was made all the more difficult when her consort,
Twilight, left her stranded on a shoal. The *Lillie Martin* got off on
her own and made it back to St. Louis by September. Near that
city some two years later she broke in two and burned. Her life
span of about four years was average for steamers of that day. The
Twilight, in the meantime, had returned to St. Louis in September,
1865, and immediately loaded for another trip up. But she hit a
snag near Sibley and sank on September 10. Not long afterward
the river shifted away from the wreckage site and she was covered
in sand and silt. At the time of her sinking, the *Twilight* had been
carrying 300 barrels of whiskey along with an assortment of iron,
lead, and steam engines meant for the Montana gold mines. Folks
living near the wreckage site never could forget about that buried
whiskey. Finally, some thirty years later, certain gentlemen in
Kansas City formed a salvage company and went after it. It proved
to be quite a chore, for the remains of the *Twilight* had settled to a
depth of thirty-nine feet under the sandy loam. After much effort
and expense the salvors brought out several bottles of an 1860 gin
and one barrel of aged whiskey. Apparently both products were
good, but not so good as to encourage more hard digging, and the
project was abandoned.

A lady's honor

Missouri River steamers carried the laws and mores of civilization to
the frontier. The transition was not always smooth. Fur traders who
had been up the river for years and were used to having things their

own way often bullied the meek travelers from the East. This especially could be the case with the *bourgeois,* the head men of the fur trading outposts. Life at those outposts was hard and uncertain and men rose to the position of *bourgeois* by main force. They were accustomed to being in charge, even when they rode the steamboats. In 1856, Joseph LaBarge was captain of a boat owned by the American Fur Company. At Fort Clark, a company outpost in the Dakota territory, the boat picked up a certain disagreeable *bourgeois.* This tyrant had been away from civilization for so long that he regarded everything, even another man's wife, to be within his grasp. The chief clerk of the boat was the son of a director of the fur company. The clerk had

CAPTAIN JOSEPH LABARGE. Born in St. Louis in 1815, LaBarge began his Missouri River career in 1836 and worked on the river as a pilot, captain, and boat owner until 1885. He was fluent in French and English, and usually wrote his logs in French. A devout Catholic, LaBarge allowed Jesuit missionaries free passage on his steamers, and named one of his last boats *DeSmet,* after Father Pierre-Jean DeSmet, whom he had known from his many trips to the upper river. LaBarge died in St. Louis in 1899.

(FROM CHITTENDEN, HISTORY OF EARLY STEAMBOAT NAVIGATION ON THE MISSOURI RIVER.)

brought his young wife along for the trip, and the clerk's father had asked LaBarge to be especially mindful of her comfort and protection. Little did LaBarge know that the clerk was more interested in advancing his own career than protecting his wife. LaBarge tells the story from the time the *bourgeois* stepped onto the boat:

When he came on board he went to the office and told the clerk to assign him a stateroom so that he could have his baggage sent to it. The clerk promised to attend to it and the *bourgeois* withdrew. The clerk and myself then looked over the register to see what we could do for him. There was only one room that could be made available except by causing passengers who had secured and paid for their rooms to vacate them. This room was occupied by two clerks, who were compelled to give it up and sleep on cots outside. It was a forward stateroom, and hence not so desirable as those farther aft, but still a good room, and the only one that was available. I directed the clerk to have the *bourgeois'* baggage put in, and to show him the room when he should request it.

About 9 p.m., when the boat was tied up for the night, and I was in the office writing up the journal, the *bourgeois* came in and asked the clerk for his room. The clerk took him out and showed him his room and told him that two of the clerks had given it up for him. The *bourgeois* turned up his nose and exclaimed, "What! That room for [me], a member of the firm. Can't I have a room in the after cabin, where the *bourgeois* are usually assigned?"

He was told that it was impossible without ousting others who could not reasonably be disturbed. He did not ask me, for he knew I would not grant it. Then drawing himself up in a pompous fashion, he said to the clerk, calling him by name: "I will occupy your room tonight and you may occupy this," and added other suggestions not calculated to mollify the feelings of the young husband.

The clerk came into the room deathly pale, but made no response to the *bourgeois'* insulting insinuations. I overheard the whole conversation, and determined to remain up and see the affair out. After a while the *bourgeois* came to the door of the office and said to the clerk, "Good night," . . . and started for the ladies' cabin. I immediately stepped out and followed him. He walked directly back to the clerk's stateroom and was about to take hold of the door knob, when I seized him by the collar, jerked him around, gave him a smart kick in the direction of the forward cabin, followed it up by two or three others, and in short order landed him in front of the boat yelling "murder," and calling for help. Culbertson and others came out, but I told them not to interfere, as I was simply protecting a lady from insult. The *bourgeois* would not be quiet, and I ordered my mate Hooper to put him on the bank. This was promptly done, the boat was held offshore by a spar, the gang plank drawn in, and the *bourgeois* could not get back on board. The weather was so warm that he would not suffer from the cold, and the pestering mosquitoes, which swarmed in the willows, kept him active all night.

When I returned to St. Louis I made no report of this affair, leaving it to the clerk, whose wife's honor had been protected, to lay the matter before his father. Instead of reporting the facts he represented that I had treated the *bourgeois* with uncalled-for severity, and that such things ought not to be allowed to go on. He said nothing of the real cause of the trouble, although his wife, a refined, cultured, and beautiful woman, drove to my house as soon as she returned, and told my wife how thankful she was for what I had done.

A few days after my return . . . was summoned to the office, and was there informed that the men in the upper country thought me altogether too hard on them, and that, to avoid future difficulty, it was best to terminate our relations. I replied that I felt so fully justified in my action that I should retire from their service with the utmost willingness if such was their view of the affair.

Three years later I was again called to the office and thus addressed by the father of my ungrateful clerk:

"I have called you in to scold you for your conduct."

"Why so, Mr. ——?"

"You remember the cause of the trouble in 1856 that led to our separation?"

"Very distinctly."

"Why did you not defend yourself? Why did you not make me a full report?"

"I thought, sir, it was your son's place to lay the matter before you, as the whole trouble had been on his and his wife's account. I had promised I would protect her, and all I did was in fulfillment of that promise. I am glad that you now know the truth of the matter."

"Perhaps you are right; it was my son's place to tell me; but he was influenced by others and never mentioned it."

The old gentleman was very indignant over the affair, and ever after treated me with the greatest consideration.

Passing the time

Three months' confinement on a small steamer while clawing up the dangerous Missouri could test anyone's patience. Mountain-bound passengers had to develop a certain stoic acceptance of their predicament and resort to diversions that were peculiar to their situation. A typical trip from the passengers' point of view is told in this excerpt from a riverman's biography:

> While the officers and crew were kept alert and active the live-long day in getting their boat up the troublesome stream, the passengers whiled away their time as best they could. Games of all practicable sorts were indulged in. It was a common pastime to stand on the forecastle or boiler deck and shoot at geese and ducks on the river. Now and then the sight of deer and other animals enlivened the moment, and occasionally the appearance of Indians on the bank caused a flutter of excitement. To relieve the tedium of the voyage it was a common thing, when there was no danger from the Indians, to land at the beginning of extensive bends, and ramble across the country to the other side, rejoining the boat when it came along.
>
> The pilothouse was the favorite resort on the boat when the condition of navigation would permit the passengers to be there. The pilot was always an interesting personage to get acquainted with. When in the proper mood and sailing along some easy stretch of river, he would unloosen his tongue and entertain his listeners with tales of his adventurous experiences, in reality the accumulated stories of many years, but as new to the tenderfoot as if told for the first time. Here he would point out a dry sand waste where the channel ran the year before and where now a fine crop of willows was shooting vigorously upward. The high bank yonder, with a grove of cottonwoods close to the water's edge, was where the boat was attacked by Indians a few years before and two of the crew killed. The holes where bullets tore through the pilothouse were still visible as tragic reminders of a hairbreath escape. A little farther on was where the boat once had to stop to let a herd of buffalo cross the river, for it would not do to try to run through the herd lest their huge bodies become entangled in the wheels and cripple it altogether. Sometimes these delays amounted to several hours. In another place the captain would point out the grave of some Indian chief reposing in the arms of a tree, where it had been placed by his people years before, and the sight would suggest many thrilling experiences, and even tragedies, which marked the intercourse of these primitive people with the navigators of the river. The recital of these traditions appealed to the imagination of the traveler, and helped allay the monotony of the voyage. If the landscape might often be likened to the "uniform view of the vacant ocean," there were nevertheless a thousand features on every trip which the most interesting ocean voyage lacks.

Among the important events of every voyage were the arrivals at the various trading posts. To the occupants of these remote stations, buried in the depths of the wilderness, shut out for months from any glimpse of the world outside, the coming of the annual boat was an event of even greater interest than to the passengers themselves. Generally the person in charge of the post, with some of the employees, would drop down the river two or three days' ride and meet the boat. When she drew near the post, salutes would be exchanged, the colors displayed, and the passengers would throng the deck to greet the crowd which lined the bank. The exigencies of navigation never left much time for celebration and conviviality. The exchange of cargo was carried on with the utmost dispatch, and the moment the business was completed the boat proceeded on her way.

Indian attack

On at least one instance hostile Indians boarded a boat and came very near to capturing the crew. It was in 1847. The boat was the *Martha,* captained by the intrepid Joseph LaBarge. According to his biographer, everything went well until the *Martha* reached the Dakota Territory:

At Crow Creek there was a band of Yankton Sioux near a trading establishment under charge of Colin Campbell. Here agent Matlock gave the Indians a feast and left part of their annuities, but not all, being induced by the company's agent to deposit the balance at Fort Pierre. The Indians were sharp enough to see that they had not received all they were entitled to and naturally could not understand why. Campbell assured them that they would receive the balance at Fort Pierre.

"Why not here?" asked the Indians. "Why make this long journey for what we can just as well get right here?"

Campbell turned them off by saying that the Indian agent could attend to the matter there better.

The Indians sullenly acquiesced, evidently much dissatisfied. Campbell had cut ten or twelve cords of wood at this place for use of the boat, but it was not needed till the down trip. Captain LaBarge feared, however, that if it was left, the Indians, in their present temper, would burn it, and he therefore concluded to take it along. The Indians refused to let the wood be taken without pay, and seated themselves on the pile so that the men could not get at it. The captain was compelled to pay for the wood, although it had been cut by company men.

But the matter did not end here. Etienne Provost, who was employed on these trips to take charge of the rough and turbulent mountain men, was asked to attend to the loading of the wood, as it was feared there might be trouble. Provost came up on the boiler deck and sat down by LaBarge, saying: "We are going to have some fun before that wood is on board." He then shouted "Woodpile! Woodpile!" and enough men rushed out to the bank to take the whole woodpile at once. Provost ordered them to pick up all they could carry and then to move on to the boat one after another, so as to have no crowding or confusion on the gangplank.

Meanwhile a dozen or more Indians were standing by, looking on. When the men were loaded up and were jammed close together in single file on their way to the boat, the Indians jumped upon them and began to belabor them with the rawhide horsewhips which they always had fastened to their waists. The men were frightened almost out of their wits, and dropping their wood, scrambled on board the best way they could. Provost lay back and roared with laughter, saying, "I told you we should see some fun."

He then went out himself onto the bank where the Indians were, and said, "Now, men, come out here and get this wood." They came and loaded up. "Now go on board," he said, and they went entirely unmolested. Provost went last, and before descending the bank, turned toward the Indians and asked them: "Why don't you stop them? Are you afraid of me?" The truth is they were afraid of him. They knew him well and respected him, and understood that he would stand no foolishness.

LaBarge thought nothing further of the affair, for the Indians soon disappeared, as he supposed, for good. The wind was too high to proceed, and the boat remained at the bank nearly all the afternoon waiting for it to subside.

"Everything quieted down," said the captain, in describing what followed, "and I was sitting in the cabin reading a paper, when all of a sudden there was a heavy volley of firearms and the sound of splintered wood and broken glass. This was instantly followed by an Indian yell and a rush for the boat, and in the uproar someone cried out that a man had been killed. The Indians got full possession of the forward part of the boat and flooded the boiler grates with water, putting out the fires. They had learned something of steam in the fifteen years that boats had been going up the river.

"My first act was to rush to my wife's stateroom, where I found Mrs. LaBarge unharmed. I told John B. Sarpy, who with his son was making the trip, to barricade her door with mattresses and to stay there until the trouble was over. I then hastened to the front of the [main] cabin, but was met at the door by the Indians. Retreating, I met Colin Campbell, and asked him what the Indians wanted. Campbell replied that they wanted me to give up the boat; that if I would do so they would let the crew go, but if I resisted they would spare no one.

"After the first rush the Indians seemed timorous and uncertain, evidently fearing some unpleasant surprise in the labyrinths of the boat. This gave me time for effective measures. I had on board a light cannon of about 2 inches caliber, mounted on four wheels. Unluckily it was at this time down in the engine room undergoing some repairs to the carriage. I had in my employ a man on whom I could absolutely rely—a brave and noble fellow, Nathan Grismore, the first engineer. Grismore had just finished the work on the cannon, and told me he thought he could get it up the back way, since the fore part of the boat was in possession of the Indians. He got some men and lines and soon hoisted the gun on deck and hauled it into the after part of the cabin. I always kept in the cabin some powder and shot for use in hunting. I got the powder, but the supply of shot was gone. Grismore promptly made up the loss with boiler rivets and the gun was heavily loaded and primed, ready for action.

"By this time the forward part of the cabin was crowded with Indians who were evidently afraid something was going to happen. I lost no time in verifying their fears. As soon as the gun was loaded I lighted a cigar, and holding the smoking stump in sight of the Indians, told Campbell to tell them to get off the boat or I would blow them all to the devil. At the same time I started for the gun with the lighted cigar in my hand. The effect was complete and instantaneous. The Indians turned and fled and fairly fell over each other in their panic to get off the boat. In less time than it takes to tell it, not an Indian was in sight. I had the cannon brought onto the roof, where it remained for an hour or more.

"As soon as the Indians were off the boat I began to look up the crew who had ingloriously fled at the first assault, leaving the boat practically defenseless. They had hidden, some here and some there, but most of them on the wheels (it was a sidewheel boat) where I found them packed thick as sardines all over the paddles. These were the brave mountaineers who were never slow in vaunting their courage and valorous performances! I was so disgusted that I was disposed to set the wheels in motion and give them all a dunking; but the fires had been put out by the Indians.

"The wind having subsided, we resumed our journey, and about a mile farther on attempted to cross to the other shore. Failing in this we encamped for the night. On the following morning we buried the deck-hand, Charles Smith, who had been killed when the attack began."

The Missouri is constantly changing its
course; wearing away its banks on one
side, while it forms new ones on the
other. Its channel is shifting continually.
Islands are formed,
and then washed away;
and while the old forests on one side
are undermined and swept off,
a young growth springs up from the
new soil upon the other.

FRANCIS PARKMAN
THE CALIFORNIA AND OREGON TRAIL

Epilogue

CHANNEL REALIGNMENT PROJECT AT INDIAN CAVE BEND,
NEAR RULO, NEBRASKA. The top photo, taken in June, 1935, shows
pile dikes recently driven into the streambed to divert the flow of water
away from the right bank. In the middle photo, taken four months later,
the river has begun to narrow and entrench itself within its bed. The lowest picture, shot in November, 1947, shows the final result: a deepened
channel and increased agricultural acreage. Scores of similar projects have
combined to make the present-day Missouri commercially navigable from
St. Louis County to Sioux City, Iowa—732 river miles.

Decline and change

Packet steamboating on the Missouri River lasted from the 1820s to the 1880s, with the greatest period of activity from 1840 to 1860. The War Between the States hastened the decline of the enterprise, inasmuch as guerrilla warfare in Missouri added a new dimension of danger to the business. Confederate guerrillas frequently targeted steamboats during the war—many boats were fired upon, a few were boarded. That alone would have been enough to discourage traffic on the river; but in addition, a number of boats that normally operated on the Missouri went south under charter to the Federal government. The Army used them as transports to supply goods to the various military campaigns in the Mississippi and Tennessee River Valleys. The rigors of wartime service wore them out.

The war alone did not kill Missouri River steamboating. Railroads contributed significantly to the demise. In the decade of the 1860s, railways caught up with the frontier. Intrastate railroads had been completed from Hannibal, Missouri, to St. Joseph; from St. Louis to Kansas City; and from Dubuque, Iowa, to Council Bluffs. And the transcontinental railroad ran from Omaha westward. All of these routes siphoned off long-haul passenger and freight business, and relegated steamboat traffic to way stops and to service on minor tributaries. In 1867, there were seventy-one steamers regularly plying the Missouri; three years later there were only nine.

Beginning in 1879 a group of investors attempted to revive the packet trade on the Missouri. They built three new boats, the *Dacotah, Wyoming,* and *Montana.* These fine boats were designed especially for the Fort Benton trade, and enjoyed a few seasons of success. The *Dacotah* made seven trips to Montana during the 1880s—on one trip up she carried 700 tons of goods. She also set the record for the largest load brought down the Missouri in a single trip: 16,000 sacks of wheat and 5,000 pieces of freight. In 1882 the *Wyoming* set an unusual record of her own—she came down from Fort Benton with the largest shipment of livestock ever transported on a steamboat: 316 head of cattle. The *Montana* made two trips to her namesake territory, then was damaged by a tornado at Bismarck. After that she ran on the lower river and sank at St. Charles, Missouri, in 1884, after hitting a bridge pier. Despite the rather spectacular early successes of these three boats, the investors lost money due to high insurance premiums and cut-throat pricing by the railroads.

For all but minor shipments of bulk freight, steamboating was dead on the Missouri by 1890. Even champions of the former packet days, such as Captain Hiram M. Chittenden of the Army Corps of Engineers, realized that the flush times were over and saw no further need to improve the river. Chittenden advocated a system of canals in the Dakotas and Nebraska to irrigate the Great Plains, knowing that the plan would draw off so much water as to preclude deep-water navigation in the lower river. A few family-owned companies continued to operate small freight boats, mostly on the Gasconade and Osage Rivers, where the railways had made few inroads. Besides freight they carried passengers on day trips and excursions. These valiant little businesses survived from season to season—always teetering on the edge of financial failure. By the 1910s they were all that remained of the great era of packet steamboating.

The Missouri would remain virtually unused until the First World War. Ironically, the railroads brought commerce back to the river, for they were unable to handle the huge demands of the national emergency. Freight cartage returned to the river, but in a mode altogether different than before. The packet boats, and the passengers, were gone. In their place came towboats pushing strings of barges—a more efficient and economical means of moving bulk commodities. This led to extensive work by the Corps of Engineers to improve navigation on the river. Through ingenious methods that took advantage of the river's own hydraulic forces, the Missouri was narrowed, deepened, and stabilized. From Montana to South Dakota, a series of dams and reservoirs was constructed to regulate flow levels on the lower river. Sioux City, Iowa, became the head of navigation.

But what of the future of Missouri River navigation? The matter is in some doubt. Farmers, environmentalists, and boatmen compete for the river's favor, each to the exclusion of the others. In truth the future of navigation on the Missouri is just as it was a century ago—tenuous and uncertain. It may be that the great days of the Missouri lie only in its past. If that is so, then there can be no regrets—it was a time well-lived and fondly remembered. Like a wistful dream, the recollection of those days gives us pause—and beckons us back—for one more look and one more ride on that wild and muddy river.

"Successful pilots on the Upper Missouri possessed rare talents. Owing to the short season, they ran the river only once or twice per year, and it never presented the same channel to them. Certainly they were a boastful lot; after all, they took their vessels up to the mountains where steamboats were never intended to go. And yet their boasts were not without merit, for there was something peculiar about the Missouri—something that warranted the quadrupling of a Mississippi pilot's pay; something that set boat builders to designing "spoonbill" bows and "bustle" sterns; something that compelled rivermen to risk everything through two thousand miles of the highest winds, lowest water, deadliest Indians, and most numerous snags of any river on the continent."

Appendix

Glossary

balance rudder—A rudder that extended both fore and aft of the rudder post. The balance rudder made steering easier and provided better response due to increased surface area of the rudder.

banking freight—The act of taking off freight from a boat and placing it temporarily onshore in order to lessen the draft of the boat. Banking freight was necessary in some instances to set free a grounded boat.

bar—A naturally occurring shallow area in or adjacent to the channel; composed of sand or sometimes gravel. In very low water, bars are exposed above the surface.

beam—The widest cross section of a boat's hull, measured internally. The term also was used to denote the midpoint of a hull's length.

bell ropes—Also known as bell cords, they were wooden-handled or brass-ringed cords strung from the ceiling of the pilothouse. The pilot used them to signal the engineer to stop, come ahead, or reverse the engine. Sidewheel boats had two sets of bell ropes—one for each engine.

boiler—The enclosed iron cylinder in which water was heated to create steam. A firebox, located beneath the boiler, heated the boiler water. Hot gases from the firebox additionally were vented through flues within the boiler. A pump replaced the water as it steamed off. The water level within the boiler was critical and usually was the contributing factor in boiler explosions. The largest steamboats had as many as eight boilers.

boiler deck—The second deck. The boiler deck was one deck above the boilers. The cabin and staterooms were located on the boiler deck.

bucket—A wooden blade, or paddle, of a paddlewheel. On larger vessels a single bucket consisted of several heavy boards bolted together.

bullboat—An elongated craft made of buffalo bull hide stretched over a framework of willow branches. Seen frequently on the Upper Missouri, especially on its western tributaries.

bustle stern—A design adaptation found on many sternwheel boats equipped with balance rudders. The bustle was a bulge in the stern below the waterline that prevented driftwood from jamming the forward throw area of the rudder.

cabin—An elongated, central room, running fore and aft, on the boiler deck. Also known as the main cabin, or parlor, it served as both the social hall and dining room for the cabin passengers. The cabin often featured an ornate motif and raised roof with skylights of colored glass. Doors to individual staterooms lined either side of the cabin. On larger boats, the barbershop, bar, and clerk's office were located in rooms at the forward end.

capstan—A large winch, or windlass, mounted vertically on a boat's forecastle. Capstans were used for pulling in heavy lines. Early in the steamboat era they were turned by hand, but in later years most boats utilized steam-powered capstans.

channel—The deepest part of the river bed. The channel is more or less continuous, but is difficult to perceive as it crosses from one side of the river to the other.

chute—The non-channel watercourse around an island. Often no more than a bayou or creek, the chute delineated the "back side" of an island. Like cutoffs, chutes could be navigated in high water by up bound boats. This usually resulted in a shorter running distance compared to the channel side.

cordelling—Towing a vessel upstream from the bank. The term dates to keelboat days. The cordelle was a heavy line attached to the keelboat mast and hauled forward by men or draft animals on shore.

cutoff—An alteration to the water course that occurred when the river cut through the narrow neck of a horseshoe-shaped bend. Natural cutoffs took place during flood stages when saturation and erosion weakened the banks, causing them to cave in and give way to the force of the moving water. Manmade cutoffs were formed by the construction of a narrow ditch across the peninsula, leaving a temporary earthen plug at either end. When the plugs were removed, the river flowed in and widened the ditch by scouring action. Given time, the river would abandon the longer path around the bend in favor of the cutoff.

cylinder head—The solid end block, or cap, of a steam piston cylinder. It was attached to the cylinder by a series of bolts and had to withstand maximum steam pressure within the cylinder without leaking or cracking.

deck passage—Equivalent to steerage class on ocean steamers, deck passage entitled the traveler to occupy only the main deck during the voyage. Meals were not included, but could be purchased individually. Shelter was minimal and often consisted of nothing more than a wide shelf upon which to make one's berth.

displacement—The weight of water moved aside, or displaced, by the hull of a boat. In order to remain buoyant, the weight of a boat could not exceed the weight of the displaced water.

doctor (engine)—A steam operated pump. Its primary purpose was to feed water into the boiler.

double—The act of making two trips past a given point, while carrying half the cargo load on each trip. This was made necessary where the current was too strong for the boat to gain headway with its full load of freight.

draft—The depth of a boat's hull under the waterline. Draft was measured at the bow and stern, and could be manipulated by shifting the cargo load fore and aft.

forecastle—The portion of the main deck that extended forward of the superstructure. The forecastle was the area for the anchors, capstan, spars, stage plank, and hawsers. It was common also to store freight in this area.

flue—One or more pipes that extended through the length of a boiler. The flue carried hot gases from the firebox to the breeching and aided in heating the water within the boiler. The flue could become red hot when exposed by low water in the boiler. This often then led to a collapse of the flue and an explosion of the boiler.

guard—That portion of the main deck that extended beyond the width of the hull. On larger boats the overhanging guards on either side increased the main deck area by several thousand square feet; this allowed a much greater cargo carrying capacity. The guards also helped deflect floating objects and fixed obstructions from the path of the side paddlewheels. It is from this function that they derived their name.

gunwale—The upper edge of the sides of the hull. The main deck guards overlapped the gunwale of most steamboats. Sometimes phonetically spelled as gunnel.

hawser—A heavy line, or rope. Used for mooring or towing a vessel.

hog chains—A system of chains and rods meant to prevent the hull from sagging, or "hogging," under heavy loads. Hog chains extended from the forward hull, up over the hurricane deck, and back down to the stern. They could be tightened or loosened as needed by means of turnbuckles.

hogshead—A wooden barrel with a liquid capacity of at least 63 gallons.

hurricane deck—The uppermost deck of a steamboat. The name was derived from the ever-present breeze that made it a favorite viewing place on warm evenings. It was the location of the boat's large signal bell.

jackstaff—A tall pole mounted on the bow. Though often depicted as a flagpole, the jackstaff served primarily as a vertical reference line to assist the pilot in aligning the bow with a point on shore. (See also *verge*.)

kedge—The act of pulling a steamboat over a shoal or bar by means of a small anchor known as the kedge. Trailing a hawser, the kedge was carried by yawl to a point beyond the shoal; it was then dropped overboard with the other end of the hawser wound around the boat's capstan. When the capstan turned, the boat was winched forward.

keel—The main structural member of the hull, running fore and aft, upon which additional framework was formed. The keel of sailing craft projected well below the lines of the hull, but it was less prominent on river steamboats. Eventually the evolution of riverboat designs led to the elimination of the protruding keel in favor of an internal longitudinal beam known as the keelson.

keelboat—A wooden freight boat built upon a keel, with a pointed bow and stern. They were propelled by means of poles, oars, or tow lines. Keelboats often exceeded sixty feet in length, with an enclosed cabin amidships.

ladies' cabin—The back, or after section, of the cabin. On some boats the ladies' cabin was partitioned off from the main cabin, on others it was delineated by the presence of fine carpeting. The ladies' cabin sometimes featured a piano and colored-glass windows facing rearward. While not the exclusive domain of women, social mores of the time dictated that a gentleman would not enter the ladies' cabin unless escorted or invited in by a woman. It also served as a family room.

larboard— The left side of a boat. Now called the port side.

lead (line)—A weighted rope with marked increments that was used to measure the river's depth. The lead line was thrown forward from near the bow and pulled taut as the boat drew alongside. The leadsman sang out the depth in a voice loud enough to be heard in the pilothouse.

lighter—A barge or old hull used to carry a portion of a steamboat's cargo. Most often a lighter was used in order to reduce the draft of the steamboat in shoal water. Usually the lighter was lashed alongside the steamboat.

lock and dam—A structure that dammed the river during periods of low water to create an artificial pool upstream, combined with facilities for permitting the passage of a boat from one water level to the other.

Mackinaw—A flat-bottomed, wooden-planked boat with a high, pointed bow and stern. Mackinaws followed the same design of sailing vessels found on the Great Lakes, and could reach forty feet in length. They carried a mast and sail, but on the river they more often were propelled by poles or tow lines. Used primarily for downriver transportation.

main deck—The lower deck of a steamboat. Most of the main deck was open space. It included areas for boilers, fuel bins, engine room, livestock pens, and freight. (See also *forecastle*.)

minie ball—A conical, hollow-backed bullet used in military rifles of the Civil War era. The name is derived from Claude-Étienne Minié, one of the developers of the projectile.

mud drum—A cylinder-shaped sump, located beneath the boilers. The mud drum was meant to collect sediment from the boiler water.

packet —A boat that carried both passengers and freight. A packet company, or packet line, consisted of mutually owned or affiliated steamboats that operated on a regular schedule.

pitman (rod)—Made of thick, layered wood with iron reinforcements, it was the connecting link between the piston rod and the paddlewheel crank. Use of the direct-connecting pitman rod replaced the walking beam.

planter—A submerged tree trunk with one end lodged in the river bottom and the upper end poised at or near the surface.

prow—The foremost, angled portion of the bow.

reef—A submerged ridge. Reefs usually angled downstream from a point of land or the head of an island. Typically, they took shape as a gradual slope that rose to within a few feet of the surface, followed by a sharp drop-off.

samson posts—A series of heavy poles over which the hog chains were strung. Samson posts extended vertically or diagonally upward from the hull and distributed the load of the hog chains evenly throughout the length of the hull.

sawyer—A submerged tree, nearly waterlogged, but with enough buoyancy to permit the upper branches to occasionally rise above the surface. The name was derived from its up and down motion.

sidewheeler—A steamer with two paddlewheels, one on either side of the boat. In all but the smallest sidewheelers, the paddlewheel was enclosed in a housing to minimize spray.

snag—An object embedded in the stream that created an obstruction or hazard to navigation. The term most especially applied to trees and limbs encountered singularly or in clusters.

snagboat—A shallow-draft, double-hulled steamboat designed to remove snags from the river channel. Removal usually was accomplished by pulling or lifting the snag from its location and then cutting it into small sections.

sounding—The act of measuring a river's depth, usually by means of a lead-weighted rope, or a pole. Depth was measured in feet up to nine feet; when deeper than nine feet it was called out at intervals of quarter-fathoms $1\frac{1}{2}$ feet per quarter-fathom; 6 feet per fathom).

spoonbill bow—A well-rounded prow, resembling the bowl of a spoon, that enabled a steamboat to beach itself at a shallow landing. The slow turning of the paddlewheels would hold the boat in place while loading or unloading, after which the boat could then extract itself by reversing the engines. Spoonbill bows were seen on many upper river boats beginning in the mid-1860s.

stage (plank)—The walkway, or gangplank, that extended from a boat's forecastle to the shore. Most boats carried a stage on either side. Stage planks were heavy and usually required the aid of a mast and boom to place them in position.

starboard—The right side of a boat. Derived from the Old English word *steorbord,* meaning "steering side."

staterooms—Sleeping rooms located on either side of the cabin. Each stateroom had an inner door leading to the cabin, and a window and outer door opening up to the boiler deck balcony. Staterooms were small with nothing more in them than a bunk bed and a wash stand and chair. Some staterooms could be enlarged by removing an interior bulkhead. The term "stateroom" supposedly is derived from the habit of naming each room after a state rather than assigning a number to it.

sternwheeler—A steamer with one large paddlewheel located at the stern.

tiller—The pivoting control arm that connected to the rudder.

transom—The abrupt, transverse closing of the stern found on sternwheelers. The transom formed a vertical wall to which the rudder posts were attached. Transoms were uncommon on sidewheelers due to the rounded closure of their sterns.

towboat—A powered craft designed to push barges. Steam era towboats were sternwheelers. Outwardly they differed in appearance from packet boats by their squared prow and towing knees (i.e., forward-facing bumpers). Internally, they were more powerful and did not carry passengers. Despite their name, towboats *pushed* barges, either ahead or alongside.

verge (-staff)—A flagpole mounted on a boat's centerline near the stern. By sighting with the jackstaff on the bow and the verge at the stern, a pilot could keep his boat aligned with points on shore.

walking beam—A fulcrum-like apparatus that transferred the up-and-down movement of the piston stroke to the circular motion of the paddlewheel shaft. Also known as a working beam, it was seen only on the earliest river steamboats.

wharfboat—A floating dock, usually built from the hull of a dismantled steamboat. They often were owned by packet lines or freight consignment companies. Nearly all of them featured warehouse storage space; some sported an upper deck with rooms for passengers awaiting a boat.

warping—The act of pulling a boat over shoal water by means of running a hawser from the boat to a fixed object on shore. The boat was then reeled forward by wrapping the hawser around the captsan.

wooding—The act of loading fuel wood onto a steamboat. Typically, wooding lasting about an hour and took place twice a day.

woodyards—Independently owned refueling sites along the river. Anyone with riverside property and access to wood for fuel could operate a woodyard. The woodyard owner cut the wood and sold it by the cord (4-ft. x 4-ft. x 8-ft. sections) at whatever price the market would bear. Some woodyard entrepreneurs loaded the wood onto flatboats so that a passing steamer could take the flat in tow and unload without stopping. After the Civil War, steamboats gradually converted to coal and the once-common woodyards disappeared from the rivers' shores.

yawl—A rowboat that served as an auxiliary craft on nearly all steamboats.

Selected Bibliography

The following articles, books, private journals, government documents, dissertations, and newspapers were consulted and used in the preparation of this book.

Audubon, Maria R., ed. *Audubon and His Journals*. 2 vols. New York: Scribner's Sons, 1897.

Blossom, Henry Martyn, Journal, 1851-1853. Missouri Historical Society Collections. St. Louis.

Bradbury, John. *Travels in the Interior of America in the Years 1809, 1810, and 1811*. Liverpool: Sherwood, Neely, & Jones, 1817.

Carroll, William F. "Arsenal Island: The Ellis Island of the West." *Westward* 7 (November 1977): 5-17.

Chappell, Phil E. "Missouri River Steamboats." *Transactions of the Kansas State Historical Society* 9 (1906): 278.

Chittenden, Hiram M. *The American Fur Trade of the Far West*. 3 vols. New York: Francis P. Harper, 1902.

_____. *History of Early Steamboat Navigation on the Missouri River: Life and Times of Joseph LaBarge*. 2 vols. New York: Francis P. Harper, 1903.

_____ and Richardson, Alfred T. *Life, Letters, and Travels of Father Pierre-Jean DeSmet, S.J., 1801-1873*. 4 vols. New York: Francis P. Harper, 1905.

Cowell, Joseph L. *Thirty Years Passed Among the Players in England and America*. New York: Harper, 1844; reprint ed., Hamden, Conn.: Archon Books, 1979.

Daily Missouri Republican [St. Louis]. 8 July 1839; 4 July 1842; 25 June 1844; 3 July 1844; 4 April 1845; and 28 February 1856.

Deatherage, Charles P. *Steamboating on the Missouri in the Sixties*. Kansas City: Alexander Printing, 1924.

Dohan, Mary H. *Mr. Roosevelt's Steamboat*. New York: Dodd, Mead & Co., 1981.

Encyclopedia USA. S.v. "Barge Lines," by Michael L. Gillespie.

Fitch, George. "The Missouri River, Its Habits, and Eccentricities Described by a Personal Friend." *The American Magazine* 53 (1907): 637-40.

Foster, Walter B., Diary, 1840-1845. Missouri Historical Society Collections. St. Louis.

Greeley, Horace. *An Overland Journey from New York to San Francisco in the Summer of 1859*. New York: Saxton, Barker & Co., 1860.

Hamilton, Thomas. *Men and Manners in America*. 2 vols. Edinburgh: William Blackwood, 1833.

Hanson, Joseph M. *The Conquest of the Missouri, Being a Story of the Life of Captain Grant Marsh*. N.p.: A.C. McClurg, 1909.

Havinghurst, Walter. *Voices on the River*. New York: Macmillan, 1964.

Heckmann, William L. *Steamboating: Sixty-Five Years on Missouri's Rivers*. Kansas City: Burton Publishing, 1950.

Hesse-Wartegg, Ernst von. *Travels on the Lower Mississippi, 1879-1880: A Memoir*. Edited and translated by Frederic Trautmann. Columbia: University of Missouri Press, 1990.

Hopkins, Arthur E. "Steamboats at Louisville and on the Ohio and Mississippi Rivers." *The Filson Club Historical Quarterly* 17 (July 1943): 146-48.

Hubbell, William D. "Reminiscences of Captain William D. Hubbell." *Richmond* [Mo.] *Conservator,* 11 March 1881 and 18 March 1881.

Hunter, Louis C. *Steamboats on the Western Rivers*. Cambridge, Mass.: Harvard University Press, 1949.

Jeffries, T. Victor. *Before the Dam Water*. Lebanon, Mo.: by the author, 1980.

Latrobe, Charles J. *The Rambler in North America*. 2 vols. London: Seeley & Burnside, 1836.

Lienhard, Heinrich. *From St. Louis to Sutter's Fort, 1846.* Edited by Erwin G. Gudde and Elisabeth K. Gudde. Norman: University of Oklahoma Press, 1961.

Nichols, George W. "Down the Mississippi." *Harper's New Monthly Magazine* 41 (June-November 1870): 835-45.

Niles National Register 66 (20 July 1844): 330-31.

"Notes of a Missouri Rambler." *Missouri Historical Society Bulletin* 3 (1946): 7-10.

Official Records of the Union and Confederate Navies in the War of the Rebellion. 30 vols. Washington: GPO, 1895-1925.

Parkman, Francis, Jr. *The California and Oregon Trail.* New York: Putnam, 1849.

Paxton, W.M. *Annals of Platte County, Missouri.* Kansas City: Hudson-Kimberly, 1897.

Petsche, Jerome E. *The Steamboat Bertrand: History, Excavation, and Architecture.* Washington, GPO, 1974.

Pope, James S. "A History of Steamboating on the Lower Missouri, 1838-1849, Saint Louis to Council Bluffs, Iowa Territory." Ph.D. dissertation, St. Louis University, 1984.

St. Joseph [Mo.] *Gazette*, 14 April 1852 and 15 May 1846.

St. Louis New Era, 11 September 1843; 4 June 1844; and 19 December 1845.

Saturday Evening News [St. Louis], 10 March 1838.

Shrader, Dorothy H. *Steamboat Legacy: The Life and Times of a Steamboat Family.* Hermann, Mo.: Wein Press, 1993.

Stevens, Walter B. *Missouri: The Center State, 1821-1915.* Chicago: S.J. Clarke, 1915.

Thorpe, Thomas B. *The Mysteries of the Backwoods; or Sketches of the Southwest.* Philadelphia: Carey & Hart, 1846.

_____. "Remembrances of the Mississippi." *Harper's New Monthly Magazine* 12 (December 1855-May 1856): 39.

Toole, K. Ross. *Montana: An Uncommon Land.* Normal: University of Oklahoma Press, 1959.

Trail, E.B., Collection, 1858-1965. Joint Collection—Western Historical Manuscript Collection and State Historical Society of Missouri Manuscripts. Columbia.

Twain, Mark. *Life on the Mississippi.* Boston: Osgood & Co., 1883.

_____. *Roughing It.* New York: Harper, 1899.

U.S. Army. Corps of Engineers. *Missouri River Navigation Charts: Kansas City, Missouri, to the Mouth.* Omaha: U.S. Army Engineer Division, 1977.

U.S. Congress. House. *Message from the President of the United States to the Two Houses of Congress.* H. Executive Doc. 2, 28th Cong., 2nd sess., 1844.

Vestal, Stanley. *The Missouri.* New York: Farrat & Rinehart, 1945.

Way, Frederick, Jr. *Way's Packet Directory.* Athens: Ohio University Press, 1983.

Wayman, Norbury L. *Life on the River.* New York: Bonanza, 1971.

Weekly Reveille 1, no. 46 (25 May 1845): 362; ibid. 2, no. 8 (1 September 1845): 475; and ibid. 2, no. 48 (8 June 1846): 886.

Index

About the Author

Even in his school days, author Michael L. Gillespie felt an affinity for history. Much of it certainly came from the town in which he grew up—Independence, Missouri.

"My boyhood home was just a block away from the Santa Fe Trail," Mike recalls, "and scarcely more than a mile from the place where Jesse James robbed a train. An easy bike ride would get me to an old steamboat landing on the Missouri River—the very site, too, where Lewis and Clark once camped. Little wonder that history had such a hold on me."

After four years in the Army, Mike earned a degree in secondary education with an emphasis in history from the University of Missouri-Kansas City. While still in college he began writing historical pieces for magazines and journals. The topics ranged from the military to railroads, with frequent forays into river history. Over several years he collected a wealth of source material on river steamboating.

Mike was particularly drawn to Missouri River steamboating because the Missouri was the one true western river—the great highway that beckoned all who dared travel to the frontier and beyond. Trappers and traders and Lewis and Clark all labored upon its waters. Plucky little steamboats loaded with emigrants and pilgrims butted their way against its sandbars and snags. From its shores stretched the Santa Fe, Oregon, California, and Mormon Trails, the Pony Express, and the transcontinental railroad.

Wild River, Wooden Boats is Mike's tribute to this majestic waterway: a collection of tales of steamboating on the Missouri and its tributaries. They tell of hitting snags, dodging bullets, witnessing explosions, and stranding on ice. They are true stories, preserved through the diaries and memoirs of those who lived the adventure, and told in their own words. It's the best kind of history—the kind that comes alive.